HERALDS of a CATHOLIC RUSSIA

Twelve Spiritual Pilgrims from Byzantium to Rome

Endorsements

"Though *Heralds of a Catholic Russia* includes figures from Romanian and Greek backgrounds, it testifies overall to a lingering awareness among thoughtful Russians that a purely national Christianity will not do. And for a (supra-national) 'universal primacy' the see of Rome is the only serious contender. But if 'Holy Russia' is to be reunited with Latin Christendom—a prospect which, with all due respect to the Virgin of Fatima, seems almost as distant today as at any time in history, many things must change. Not least among them is any suggestion, in ecclesiastical words or deeds, that the Petrine office legitimately exalts the charismatic judgment of the office-holder over docility to the patrimony of Church Tradition."

— Fr. Aidan Nichols
Author of *Theology in the Russian Diaspora* and
Rome and the Eastern Churches: A Study in Schism

"In a time when many Catholics feel disaffected with their own Church—when a fair number of them are thinking, perhaps, that the grass looks greener in the Orthodox world—this collection of stories reminds us of how blessed we are to reside in the One Church that possesses the fullness of truth, a truth preserved by the structure established by Christ Himself. It can be a great antidote for any of us who take our patrimony for granted to read of men and women who have followed the truth, often at great sacrifice, and have come home to Catholicism so as to be 'better Orthodox.'"

— John-Mark L. Miravalle, SThD
Professor of Systematic and Moral Theology,
Mount St. Mary's Seminary, Maryland

"The witness of Russian and Greek Orthodox reconciled to the Church is remarkable testimony for the need of a Papal Primacy of universal authority in the Church for the unity of truth, the unity of Revelation and the visible unity of the Church as taught in Vatican I and II."

— Dennis Bonnette, PhD
Professor of Philosophy (Retired),
Niagara University

"James Likoudis is a noted Catholic writer on the separated Eastern Churches. There is much to be learned from his stirring accounts of Easterners who embraced their true home, the Catholic Church."

— The Rev. Ray Ryland, PhD, JD[†]
Author of *Drawn from Shadows Into Truth*

"These collected accounts of twelve spiritual pilgrims seeking truth cry out with particular urgency for the end of the tragic Byzantine Greco-Slav Schism. They give new reason that Our Lady of Fatima prophesied a future Catholic Russia."

— Fr. Edouard Perrone

"Vatican II responded to Our Lady of Fatima's prophecy of the conversion of Russia in an unexpected and unprecedented way by restoring a traditional and ecumenical relationship with our separated eastern brethren. Perhaps more than any other author in modern times, Mr. James Likoudis has implemented this vital aspect of the Council in his own life - from his own conversion and his tireless efforts at healing the old schism between east and west. The new edition of *Heralds of a Catholic Russia* shows how the conversion of Russia is already happening in the hearts of these pilgrims. Fatima teaches us that God uses His little ones to accomplish His designs, and this book tells the story of twelve men and women who were willing to become little ones for the sake of the One True Church."

— Timothy S. Flanders
Author of *City of God vs. City of Man: The Battles of the Church from Antiquity to the Present*

HERALDS *of a* CATHOLIC RUSSIA

Twelve Spiritual Pilgrims from
Byzantium to Rome

JAMES LIKOUDIS

REVISED EDITION

Foreword by Robert Fastiggi PhD
Edited by Andrew Likoudis

BLUE ARMY PRESS
Washington, New Jersey

First Edition ©2016 James Likoudis
Revised Edition ©2023 James Likoudis
Published 2023

All rights reserved

No part of this book may be used or reproduced in any manner whatsoever except in the case of reprints in the context of reviews, without written permission of the World Apostolate of Fatima, USA / Our Lady's Blue Army, P.O. Box 976, Washington, NJ 07882

Printed in the United States of America.
Library of Congress Control Number: 2023919857
ISBN: 979-8-9886377-2-1

Cover design and text design by Sundae Graphic Design

Published in the United States by Blue Army Press,
World Apostolate of Fatima, USA
P.O. Box 976
Washington, NJ 07882
www.bluearmy.com

Dedication

In loving memory of my beloved son, Catholic journalist Paul Augustine Likoudis (1954–2016), who loved European history.

In gratitude for my grandson, Andrew Likoudis, without whose impetus to preserve my writings, this republishing would not have occurred.

To the everlasting memory of Demetrios Kydones, 14th century Byzantine Greek disciple of St. Thomas Aquinas; of Bessarion, Archbishop of Nicaea and Cardinal of the Holy Roman Church, indomitable champion of the Council of Florence who labored indefatigably for the reconciliation of separated Eastern Churches with the Apostolic See of Peter; and of the Hellenic Greek Catholics and Russian Catholics of the Byzantine Rite who retained their venerable traditions to pray and work to end the tragic Schism.

To Pope Pius XII, the Angelic Shepherd, and hopefully a future saint and Doctor of the Church, who sought on every occasion to encourage the union of the Catholic and Orthodox Churches, to comfort and strengthen Christians suffering persecution and oppression from the totalitarian regimes of the 20th century, and defended the divine Primacy of Peter's See as essential to the Unity of the Church:

> It must not be thought that [Christ's headship and direction] of the Church is limited to an invisible or extraordinary manner; quite the contrary. The Divine Redeemer also governs his Mystical Body in a visible and ordinary way through his Vicar on earth. For all men know, Venerable Brothers, that Christ the Lord, after He had Himself in a visible way governed His 'little flock' in His mortal life, at the moment when He was to leave the world and return to His Father, committed to the Prince of the Apostles the visible direction of the entire society founded by Him. He who was so wise could not leave without a visible head the social body He had founded. Neither can it be asserted to deny this truth, that by a Primacy of jurisdiction established within the Church the Mystical Body had been provided

with a double head. For Peter, by virtue of the Primacy, is only the Vicar of Christ, and there is consequently only one principal Head of this Body, namely Christ. It is He who, without ceasing to govern the Church in a hidden manner by Himself, nonetheless rules the Church in a visible manner by him who takes His place on earth, for after His glorious Ascension into heaven, the Church rests not only on Him, but also on Peter as on a visible foundation. That Christ and His Vicar form only one single Head, Our predecessor of immortal memory, Boniface VIII, solemnly taught in his Apostolic Letter *Unam Sanctam* and his successors have never ceased to repeat it after him.

Therefore, they are in dangerous error who think that they can attach themselves to Christ the Head of the Church, without adhering faithfully to His Vicar on earth. For those who would remove the visible Head of the Church and break the bonds of visible unity, obscure and deform the Mystical Body of the Redeemer, so that it cannot be seen or recognized by men who seek the port of eternal salvation."[1]

In honor of Blessed Leopoldo of Castelnovo, Apostle of Unity between East and West.

And to the late Pope Benedict XVI, who in continuing St. Pope John Paul II's call for the "purification of memories," vigorously pursued Vatican II's path of ecumenism whose aim is "visible unity among divided Christians," a gift of God that comes to us only from the Father through His Son in the unity of the Holy Spirit.

---

[1] Pope Pius XII, Encyclical on the Mystical Body of Christ, *Mystici Corporis Christi*, (June 29, 1943).

Table of Contents

Foreword by Robert Fastiggi PhD 11

Editors Preface 15

Introduction 17

Chapter I—Madame Swetchine (1782–1857) 27

Chapter II—Count Gregory Petrovitch Schouvalov (1804–1859) 35

Chapter III—Ivan Sergeivich Gagarin, SJ (1814–1882) 45

Chapter IV—Vladimir Soloviev, "the Russian Newman" (1853–1900) .. 57

Chapter V—Princess Elizabeth Volkonskaia (1836–1897) 69

Chapter VI—Blessed Leonid Feodorov (1879–1935) 77

Chapter VII—Dr. Irene Posnov (1914–1997) 87

Chapter VIII—Venerable Vladimir Ghika (1873–1954) 99

Chapter IX—Helle Elpiniki Georgiadis (1916–1996) 107

Chapter X—Helene Iswolsky (1896–1975) 117

Chapter XI—Count George Bennigsen (1879–1962) 127

Chapter XII—James Likoudis (1928– 145

Postscript—*On the Unity of the Church and the Conversion of Russia Prophesied by Our Lady of Fatima* 191

Foreword

The stories told in the present volume make for inspirational and fascinating reading. They reveal how an honest search for the true Church of Christ led twelve different Byzantine Orthodox pilgrims to embrace the See of Rome as "the pearl of great price." While several books in recent years have traced the road to Rome on the part of Protestant and Evangelical Christians, this is the first book that I know of that shows how prayer and study—along with the guidance of the Holy Spirit—have led some outstanding Orthodox intellectuals to enter into full Catholic communion.

I have been privileged to know Dr. James Likoudis for over 27 years. In September 2019, I—along with several other colleagues—recommended him for an honorary doctorate from Sacred Heart Major Seminary in Detroit, Michigan. In my letter of recommendation, I highlighted his outstanding scholarly contributions to the defense of the Primacy and Infallibility of the Roman Pontiff. Defending the Catholic dogma of Papal Primacy has been a life-long mission of Dr. Likoudis ever since his entrance into full Catholic communion in 1952. His firm belief in the authority of the Roman Pontiff is expressed in numerous books, including *Ending the Greek Byzantine Schism* (1992), *The Divine Primacy of the Bishop of Rome and Modern Eastern Orthodoxy: Letters to a Greek Orthodox on the Unity of the Church* (2023), and *Eastern Orthodoxy and the See of Peter: A Journey Towards Full Communion* (2006).

The present book, *Heralds of a Catholic Russia*, adds a more personal touch to the dogma of Papal Primacy. It provides stories of twelve Eastern Orthodox Christians—including Dr. Likoudis himself—who came to recognize the divinely-established Primacy of the Roman Pontiff. Some of the people covered, such as Vladimir Soloviev, might be familiar to readers. The other men and women highlighted in this book, however, deserve to be better known.

In his introduction to *Heralds of a Catholic Russia*, Dr. Likoudis provides a brief but illuminating overview of the history of the Byzantine Greco-Slav Churches and the tragedy of their split from the Apostolic See of Rome. Sadly, many of these Churches came under the influence of what the great Italian scholar, Aurelio Palmieri, calls "narrow-minded nationalism." The stories of the Greek, Romanian, and Russian Orthodox covered in this volume testify to the heartfelt need for what Likoudis calls "the Church's center of visible unity, the See of Peter at Rome."

The need for communion with the Roman Pontiff is also part of the Fatima message. In chapter XIII, which serves as a postscript, Dr. Likoudis notes that the message of Fatima speaks of Russia's errors being spread. The apparitions of Fatima began just before the Bolshevik/Communist takeover of Russia in the fall of 1917. The Blessed Mother's request for the Holy Father to consecrate Russia to her Immaculate Heart shows her love for the Russian people and her recognition of Papal authority. The conversion of Russia, however, will not be complete until there is full communion with the Roman Pontiff. Fr. Joaquin Maria Alonso, CMF, one of the leading experts on Fatima, wrote: "Sr. Lucia has always thought that the conversion of Russia is not to be understood as being the return of the Russian people to the Orthodox Christian religion, rejecting the Marxist atheism of the Soviets, but rather as a total and perfect conversion to the one, true Roman Catholic Church."

In her book *"Calls" from the Message of Fatima*, Sr. Lucia confirms what Fr. Joaquin says. Speaking of the need for full Catholic communion, Sr. Lucia writes:

> We must believe in the Church, trust in it, respect it, love it, pay heed to its teaching, follow in its footsteps, and remain united with its Head, who is Christ in the person of the Supreme Pontiff of Rome, the one true Vicar of Christ on earth, head of the Mystical Body of Christ of which we are all members by our faith in Christ. . . .[2]

The need for communion with the Roman Pontiff has become all the more apparent in recent years in view of the tensions and divisions between the various Eastern Orthodox Churches. In spite of the sins

---

2 Sr. Lucia, *"Calls" from the Message of Fatima* (St Louis: The Ravengate Press, 2000), 69.

of her members, the Catholic Church—under the Roman Pontiff and the Bishops in communion with him—remains the only subsistence of the One, Holy, Catholic, and Apostolic Church on earth.[3]

The consecration of Russia to the Immaculate Heart of Mary is ultimately a call for complete conversion to the One, Holy, Catholic, and Apostolic Church. The need for full Catholic communion under the Roman Pontiff is the teaching of Vatican II[4]—even though salvation may be possible for non-Catholics lacking full knowledge. The twelve stories in this book introduce us to the "heralds of a Catholic Russia." They reveal how the Holy Spirit was moving in the hearts and minds of Byzantine Orthodox Christians during the 19th and 20th centuries to show how full communion with the See of Rome is the will of Christ and His all-holy Mother. These heralds point to a Catholic Russia, a Russia which will be a great blessing for the universal mission of the Catholic Church.

Robert Fastiggi, PhD
Bishop Kevin M. Britt Chair of Dogmatic Theology and Christology, Sacred Heart Major Seminary, Detroit, Michigan

---

3 Vatican II, *Lumen Gentium* (Vatican: 1964), no. 8.
4 Ibid., 14.

Editor's Preface

Heralds of a Catholic Russia: Twelve Spiritual Pilgrims from Byzantium to Rome documents the stories of twelve individuals who made the intellectual journey from Orthodoxy to Catholicism. These figures include scholars, clergy, and royalty, from the well-known figure Vladimir Soloviev, "The Russian Newman," to the lesser-known Ecumenist Helle Georgiadis. A final profile recounts the conversion story of my grandfather James Likoudis. These varied accounts serve as a powerful testament to the diverse ways Christ meets us along our pilgrimage, and their witness gives hope for the fulfillment of Christ's prayer "that all may be one." (John 17:21)

The book concludes with a postscript *On the Unity of the Church and the Conversion of Russia Prophesied by Our Lady of Fatima*, which has become especially significant for us today in light of the conflict between Russia and Ukraine, and the inevitable difficulties following from it. This final chapter dispels any illusions that the consecration of Russia to the Immaculate Heart of Mary requested by Our Lady to Sister Lucia was not fulfilled by the collegial consecration of Russia and the world, solemnly carried out by the Holy Pontiff St. John Paul II in 1984. However, it is also noteworthy to acknowledge the more recent consecration of Russia and the world accomplished by the Holy Father Pope Francis in March of 2022, which can only serve to call forth a greater abundance of graces from our Blessed Lady, the *Theotokos*.

It has been my great honor to edit this book and to be able to present it to you, the reader. I am especially grateful to my grandfather for entrusting me with this privileged task. The effort has not been without its difficulties, but the timing of this republication could not be more critical, as the potential impact of widespread conversion in Eastern Europe could not be more necessary than it is today, in terms of the impact it would inevitably have on the culture, and on the social and political landscape by proximity.

It is hoped that this book will serve as an impetus for those on the fence regarding religion, to take the most worthwhile risk for faith; that it serve to help Eastern Orthodox taking a closer look at the Catholic Church and her teachings, especially regarding Papal Primacy and Infallibility; that it will inspire all to contribute to greater dialogue and understanding among long-separated brethren, if not for the greater good of holiness, at least for the sake of peace; and that it will promote greater unity among all those who seek to build up the Kingdom of God in our world, and for the world to come.

Ut Unum Sint!

Andrew Likoudis
Feast of the Conversion of St. Paul
January 25, 2023
Octave of Prayer for Christian Unity

Introduction

There is no question that the Petrine supremacy of the Pope was and remains the major obstacle to the restoration of full ecclesiastical communion between Rome and the separated Byzantine Greco-Slav churches. The centuries-old Schism between Rome and the Eastern patriarchal churches, which followed Constantinople in breaking communion with the See of Peter, is the most tragic of all the schisms in the history of the Church. *The effects of that schism were to occupy the minds of the twelve spiritual pilgrims whose stories are told in this volume.* Prayer and study led them to accept that the reunion of the Greek and Russian churches with the Church of Rome, and of their Bishops with the Bishop of Rome, was—in God's plan—an essential requisite and condition for visible membership in the One Church founded by the Lord of History.

The historical weight of the Byzantine Greco-Slav Schism, which confronted the pilgrims in this book, is unintelligible, however, without some understanding of Byzantine history itself. A summary is here provided the reader with a limited understanding of a magnificent Byzantine Christendom resulting from the Emperor Constantine's moving the capital of the Roman Empire eastward to his newly founded city of Constantinople.

The Eastern Roman (Byzantine) Empire (the *"basileia ton Rhomaion"*) lasted a thousand years from the 6th century under the Emperor Justinian I to the fall of Constantinople in 1453 under its last Catholic Emperor, Constantine XI. This empire had its political, social, cultural, and religious center in Constantinople. Containing the bulk of the peoples of Eastern Christendom, it constituted a unique historical complex of Classical Greek culture involving language, literature, and philosophy; the preservation of Roman law and government; and possessing a profound Christian character drawing upon the patristic theology and monastic spirituality of the great Greek Fathers of the early Church. In the Byzantine Empire there originally flourished the patriarchates of Alexandria, Antioch, Constantinople, and Jerusalem, whose history in the first eight centuries would see great theological struggles to preserve the Church's orthodox Trinitarian and Christological teachings against widespread heresies. With Islam's conquest of the other patriarchates in North Africa and the Near East, the patriarch of Constantinople became the leading ecclesiastical figure in the Byzantine Greek world. In the 5th century under the Emperor Justinian I, the Church had become, in effect, a State-Church dominated by the emperor who was regarded as a priest-king ruling over God's chosen people and obliged to act as God's vicar to take care of both the spiritual and temporal well-being of his subjects. The patriarch of Constantinople was often the instrument of the emperor's political policies, and Byzantine ecclesiastics generally bowed to the will of the emperor, conceding to him the right to administer and manage the Church. The emperor deposed or demoted patriarchs, arranged diocesan boundaries, enforced ecclesiastical laws and discipline, and convoked councils. A deeply religious people identified Orthodoxy with the fortunes of the Byzantine Empire.

It was this politico-religious complex of Byzantine civilization priding itself on its cultural superiority (evident in art, iconography, classical and patristic literature) that would be spread among newly converted Russians and Balkan Slavs. Also imported was the Byzantine sense of doctrinal and liturgical orthodoxy after Constantinople and other patriarchs proceeded to break ecclesiastical communion with Rome and the West. It was in the 12th century that the first Byzantine Greek denials of the Roman Primacy of universal authority took place, and a formal schism with the increasingly hated Latins began to be consolidated, fueled by political and religious animosities. From that time on, despite the temporary reunion of the Roman and Byzantine Churches at the Councils of Lyons (1274) and Ferrara-Florence (1439), it was the renewed accusation of "heresy" and "Papal scandal" that were used to justify the Byzantine Greek and Russian Orthodox's continued rejection of the Successor of Peter's universal jurisdiction in and over the Universal Church. To this day, for Byzantine Orthodoxy, it is the Catholic dogmas of Papal supremacy and infallibility which remain the one persistent "sign of contradiction" impeding the restoration of their full and visible communion with the Catholic Church.

This rejection is the basic defect in Eastern Orthodox ecclesiology reflecting a departure from the traditional belief held by Christians in the first Millennium of the Church's history and which drew the attention of the spiritual pilgrims noted in this volume. By the grace of God, they were enlightened to realize that Christ the Lord had established a visible Church with a visible head in the person of the Chief and Head of the Apostles, Peter, and his successors, the Bishops of Rome. Unity in Christ is thus assured by unity with those he set over the Church to rule and guide it. It is their witness to the fullness of faith in the Catholic Church that remains an inspiration for all called to further that genuine ecumenism called forth by the Second Vatican Council (1962–65), that is, to extend the true universality of the Church and its perfect Unity, both internal and external, to all those who profess to be followers of Christ.

One of the most informed Catholic theologians of the 19th century on the history and doctrines of the Eastern Orthodox Churches was Aurelio Palmieri.[5][6] An acute observer of the political, social, and religious life of Czarist Russia, he noted in an article in the 1917 *The Catholic World*[7] that it is,

> Unity that is the label of the genuine Church of Christ. It is the most visible of her distinguishing traits. The Church's unity reveals itself in oneness of doctrine, of ministry [and worship], and of government. On earth the Church enjoys an intellectual life, for she is the living body of the divine Teacher; a pastoral life, for she carries on the redeeming work of the divine Saviour; and a social life, for she applies the maxims of the divine Civilizer. Only in the Catholic Church do we realize that *triple unity of doctrine, of ministry, of magisterium*. It is only in the Catholic Church

---

[5] Sergio Marcanzin, *Aurelio Palmieri ed il suo Contributo alla Conoscena dell'Oriente Cristiano: Un pioniare dell' ecumenismo* (Roma: *Pontificio Instituto Orientale*, 1988).

[6] For Palmieri's comprehensive examination of Eastern Orthodox theology and ecclesiology, see: his tome *Theologia Dogmatica Orthodoxa*, vols. I and II, (Florentiae: *Libreria Editrica Fiorentina*, Via del Corso, 1911), 3.

[7] Aurelio Palmieri, *The Glories of the Catholic Church* (*The Catholic World*, vol. 106, December 17, 1917), 314–320.

that Christian thought reflects the rays of the wisdom of Christ; that the Christian heart beats in unison with the heart of Christ, or rather, forms one heart with Him; and lastly, it is only in the Catholic Church that Christian souls are fully joined in a perfect social organism, whose Head is Jesus Christ Our Lord. In this way, the divine unity of the Catholic Church conveys to us the fullness of doctrinal, sacramental, and social life. The Catholic Church is truly one mind, one heart, and one soul. All the chords of her multifarious life vibrate in perfect harmony.

The teaching of the Catholic Church is a link of continuity between the past and present generations. The beliefs of the Apostolic age reecho faithfully in the Creed which we repeat devoutly in our churches today. The Catholic Church knows, by the experience of the past and her faith in the future, that the doctrinal foundations laid by Our Lord cannot be shaken by seducers. The sacraments are the channels of the divine life which flows from the heart of Christ. Outside of the Catholic Church, sacramental life has lost or impaired the unity of Christian communities. Even the Eastern Churches, although firmly clinging to the traditional teaching of Christian antiquity, have made innovations in their sacramental life.

The Catholic Church alone is endowed with the most perfect unity of government. Because of that unity, an Anglican divine called her the backbone of Christianity. That unity is not a human unity. If it were, the waves of time and the hatred of men had long since swept it away. The Catholic Church claims that Jesus Christ is her invisible Head, and the source of her spiritual life. But being a visible society among men, claiming the right to lead them to the attainment of their supernatural aims, she needs also a visible head.

If the Church is a perfect body, *unus homo, vir perfectus, Christus et Ecclesia,* according to St. Augustine,[8] Her natural perfection requires a visible head. The grossest inconsistency of those who deny the Catholic notion of the Church, consists in their denial of a supreme visible head to the mystical body of Christ.

If the Church is really that mystical body; if she lies among men in a visible society, we cannot conceive her as lacking a visible head. If St. Paul rightly compares the Church to the perfect man, and if in man the invisible soul, the source of his inward and outward life, does not preclude a visible head for the beauty and perfection of his human body, so neither does Jesus Christ, the source of the supernatural life of the Church, deprive her of a visible head. It is inconsistent, I repeat, to admit that the Church is a visible body, and at the same time, to deny to that body the most important of its visible parts. If the Church has been instituted by Christ as a perfect society, she ought to have that root of social unity and order, viz., a supreme ruler. Anarchy is the corrosive acid of society. And the Church, as a perfect society, cannot have anarchy as the foundation of her social life. Outside of the Catholic Church we find all the symptoms of rapid dissolution or of lifeless inertia. The intellectual life of Christianity has been brought to a standstill by the Churches which have broken their bond of allegiance to Rome, or it has lost its powers in the maze of rationalistic conceits. On the one hand, nationalism with the narrowness of its spirit and its bounded interests, has loosened the ties of a unity which in the Catholic Church levels all national frontiers; on the other, the revolt against Rome has culminated in the most anarchical individualism, in the disruption of the unity of the intellectual life of the Church. In Eastern Orthodoxy, the unity of the Church has been lost with profit to the

---

[8] St. Augustine, *Enarr. In Psalmos,* 18: 10.

political powers; in the Western Reformation that same unity has been dissolved to the profit of egotistical aims. While both in the East and the West, the Catholic Church stands firm in divine unity against the assaults of a narrow nationalism and of an anarchical individualism.

By nationalism, the Orthodox Churches have sunk to the level of mere tools in the hands of political power. Nationalism has been the great weakness and the great sin of the Byzantine Church, the mother of the so-called autonomous churches of the East. It has also been the grave of the Byzantine hierarchy. When the Byzantine Church shared in the life of the whole body of Christ, when her councils and Bishops turned their gaze to the West, and in their times of trial heeded the voice of Rome she enjoyed the fullness of youthful energy. By the genius of her doctors, she unfolded the treasures of divine truth; by the labors of her apostles, she enlarged the Kingdom of Christ.

Her decay begins with the ascendancy of a narrow-minded nationalism, which applied to the political and religious life of Byzantium the old saying: *'He who is not Greek is barbarian.'* In proportion as the underhand rebellion against Rome spread in the ranks of the Byzantine hierarchy, the despotism of the Basileis and their encroachments in the realm of religious life grew stronger. Some Byzantine writers claimed for their emperors the right of a supreme and uncontrolled power in every department of the life of the nation. Even the laws of rhetoric and grammar were to be promulgated by them. Nationalism infected the very roots of the Byzantine spirit, and when its work was complete, the religious schism, which had been brewing for centuries, became definite. The defection of the Eastern Churches from Rome culminated in the disintegration of Christian unity, and in the consequent ruin was undermined the authority of the Byzantine hierarchy, itself responsible for the consummation of the Eastern schism.

To justify her revolt against Rome, the Byzantine Church appealed to the theory of the legitimacy of national autonomous Churches; while, grossly inconsistent, she wished to keep under her sway the Slavic barbarians converted to Christianity by Byzantine missionaries. She did not foresee that the nationalistic theories laid down by her Patriarchs, in the course of time, would be evolved to the utmost consequences by their successors. In the 15th century, the Russian Church proclaimed her full independence from the Patriarchate of Constantinople. In the 19th century her example was followed by the Orthodox Churches of the Balkan States. Even the redeemed Greeks of the Hellenic Kingdom refused to acknowledge the supreme authority of the so-called ecumenical Patriarch, whose authority extends at present over less than five million souls. (Today, there are only a handful of Greeks left in Constantinople/Istanbul with the Patriarch's influence extending over some seven million in large Greek communities outside of Greece.)

It was in vain that, in 1871, when the Bulgarians succeeded in establishing a national Church, the Greek hierarchy, in a synod held in Constantinople, anathematized the principle of nationalism as being in direct opposition to the universal spirit of the Church of Christ, and its visible unity. In so doing, that synod condemned the doctrinal foundations of the Byzantine Church and did homage to the Catholic principle of Christian unity. The lack of that unity is the chronic disease of the Eastern Churches separated from Rome. They form an agglomeration of acephalous communities which Khomiakov (19th century Russian lay theologian) declared bound to each other by the ties of charity, but which in fact feel for each other only national hatred. As a consequence of this fearful malady, the Eastern Orthodox Churches have lost their power of resistance. They have been turned into political churches; they are all subject to political powers. Their prosperity or decay depends upon the victory or defeat of the political factions which lend them support; their life is bound to the life of the state. They are national churches, and a national church is a captive one, one separated from the Universal Church of Christ, who has thrown off the yoke of Christ on earth merely to accept the yoke of a political ruler. Rebellion against the visible ecclesiastical authority has enslaved the particular churches of the East to a visible political authority. Hence, we may rightly infer that the principle of a visible and central power in the Church, the principle of cohesion in its visible organism, comes from God, not from man. As to the fate of the Eastern autonomous Churches, we can repeat the stirring words of a noble Russian lady, Princess Elizabeth Volkonskaia, in a book which may be called the diary of her conversion to the Catholic Church:

> All the Orthodox Churches appeal to their faith in the One, Catholic and Apostolic Church. None of them, however, realized that appeal, and all together do not constitute the Church of their dreams, for their agglomeration lacks a centre of unity, by virtue of which all the parts are joined into a perfect body, which is the cause of their organic unity. They believe in the one and universal Church, I repeat; but they believe in it as in an earthly institution which in reality never exists. They have cast away one of the foundations of the Church. They have broken their relations with the centre of unity. That is the reason for their helplessness. No power in the world is able to heighten their value, to strengthen their authority, for what is human and temporary cannot support what is everlasting. We went away from the Universal Church; we cut ourselves from her life. Since the age of the separation of the East from the Apostolic See, the Eastern Churches have

no voice to speak the language of truth. Their cloisters no longer lighten the world. Social life evolves and makes progress, while they sleep profoundly. Still more, they are buried in the sepulchral darkness of sterility. Their teaching is lifeless and vague.[9]

[The erudite Italian theologian went on to observe that] The Catholic Church not only mourns over the divisions of Christianity. She labors and prays for the restoration of her primitive unity. Of herself she says with St. Basil: 'It would be monstrous to feel pleasure in the schisms and divisions of the Churches, and not to consider that the greatest good consists in the [visibly] knitting together of the members of Christ's body.'[10]

The following sons and daughters of the Greek, Russian, and Romanian Churches who became Catholics and whose lives are all too briefly given in this study came to realize that the Byzantine Greco-Slav Schism was totally unjustified. They became aware that the reasons given for maintaining a disastrous separation from the Church's center of visible unity, the See of Peter at Rome, were without merit. Coming from different perspectives, they present fascinating accounts of the working of grace in their lives and the reasons which prompted them to come to the fullness of faith maintained by the Catholic Church. In the following pages, they are shown responding to the counsel of the Prince of the Apostles: "Always be prepared to make a defense to anyone who calls you to account for the hope that is in you. Yet do it with gentleness and reverence." (1 Peter 3:15)

—**James Likoudis**

---

9 Ibid, 320, quoting from her O Tsersvki ("Essay on the Church").
10 Ibid., 326.

Chapter I

Madame Swetchine (1782–1857)
Sophie-Jeanne Soymonov Swetchine

Madame Swetchine was one of the most extraordinary women of the early 19th century who had knowledge of some of the most interesting characters who graced the brilliant imperial court at St. Petersburg.[1] She would become known later as the saintly Russian of Paris for her charitable works and salon at Number Seventy-One, Rue Saint Dominique. There she hosted the intellectual Catholic literary, political, and ecclesiastical elite. There were seen such celebrities as the Count Montalembert, Chateaubriand, Tocqueville, Donoso Cortes, Victor Cousin, Pere Gratry, Dom Gueranger, Bishop

---

[1] Sources for Madame Swetchine's life: M.J. Rouet de Journel, SJ, *Une Russe Catholique* (Paris: Desclée De Brouwer, 1953); Count De Falloux, *Life and Letters of Madame Swetchine* (New York: The Catholic Publication House, 1869) and *The Writings of Madame Swetchine* by the same author, trans by H.W. Preston (Boston: Roberts Brothers, 1870); and *Madame Swetchine: Journal De Sa Conversion* pub. Count De Falloux, (Paris: Auguste Vaton, Librarie-Editeur, 1863).

Dupanloup, Père de Ravignan, the Abbé Bautain, the Russian Jesuit Ivan Gagarin, and the great Dominican orator Lacordaire with whom she had a special friendship.[2]

Born into a noble family in Moscow, Madame Swetchine was the daughter of Peter Alexandrovich Soymonov, the secretary of state and close advisor to Catherine II. Spending her early years at the imperial court, she received a good education in all subjects except religion (though formally Russian Orthodox). Possessing a precocious intelligence, by the age of fourteen she was fluent in Russian, English, French, German, and Italian, and though not a beauty (she was rather plain), her serene, sweet, and charming character made her a favorite at court. At fifteen, she was made a lady-in-waiting to the Empress Marie Feodorovna, the wife of Czar Paul I who had succeeded Catherine II. The winning grace of her manners fascinated all who came into contact with her, and she had many suitors. At the age of seventeen in obedience to her father, she married a distinguished general, Nicholas Sergeyevich Swetchine, who was twenty-five years her senior, and whom she loved and never regretted marrying. The death of her father and knowing that she would not be able to bear children led Madame Swetchine to engage in the study of literature, philosophy, and science, and to read prodigiously to further her intellectual development. Her increasing interest in religion focused on the struggle between Christianity and the Enlightenment philosophers. She became acquainted with French emigres including Jesuits and other priests that had fled from the horrors of the French Revolution to take refuge in Russia where they established schools. Their influence resulted in a number of prominent conversions among the aristocracy to the Catholic Church.

Traveling throughout Russia in 1839 the French Catholic Marquis de Custine was an astute (if sometimes harsh) observer of Russian manners, Russian despotism, and the enslaved state of the Russian Church whose weaknesses he could not fail to observe:

---

2 *The Russian Journals of the Marquis De Custine: Journey for Our Time* (Ed. and trans. by Phyllis Penn Kohler (Chicago: Henry Regnery Company, A Gateway Edition, 1951), 254–256.

Since the usurpation of the temporal authority, the Christian religion in Russia has lost its spiritual value. It is stationary; it is one of the wheels of despotism—nothing more. In this country where nothing is neatly defined, purposely so, one has trouble in understanding the true relations of the church with the Chief of State who has made himself the arbiter of the faith, without however positively proclaiming this prerogative; he has arrogated it to himself, he exercises it in fact, but he does not dare claim it as a right. He has kept a synod—his is a final homage rendered by tyranny to the King of Kings and to His ruined Church. . . . In our time, the Russian people are the firmest in religious belief of all the Christian peoples; you have just seen the principal cause of the negligible efficacy of their faith. When the Church abdicates freedom, it loses moral potentiality; the slave gives birth only to slavery. One cannot repeat this enough, the only veritably independent Church is the Catholic Church which, alone, has thus conserved the trust of true charity; all the other churches form a constitutive part of the States which use them as political means to support their power. These churches are excellent auxiliaries of the government; complaisant toward the holders of temporal power, princes or magistrates, hard toward their subjects, they call the Divinity to the aid of the police; the immediate result is certain, it is good order in society. But the Catholic Church, just as powerful politically, comes from higher and goes further. National churches make citizens; the Universal Church makes men.

In Russia, I saw one Christian church, which no one attacks, everyone respects at least in appearance—a church that everything favors in the exercise of its spiritual authority; yet this church has no power over hearts; it can only make hypocrites or superstitious beings. In countries where religion is not respected, it is not responsible, but here, where all the prestige of an absolute power aids the priest in the accomplishment of his duties, where

> the doctrine is attacked neither by the written nor by the spoken word, where religious practices are, so to speak, imposed by the law of the State, where customs serve it as they oppose it in France, one has the right to reproach the Church for its sterility. This church is dead. However, to judge from what is happening in Poland, it can become a persecutor, whereas it has neither enough spiritual virtues nor enough great talent to conquer through the mind. In a word, the Russian Church lacks the same thing that is lacking in everything in that country: liberty, without which the spirit of life disappears, and the light goes out.
>
> Western Europe is not aware of all the religious intolerance that enters into Russian policy. The cult of the reunited Greeks has just been abolished following long and secret persecutions: does Catholic Europe know that there are no more Uniates [Christians of an Eastern rite acknowledging the Pope's Primacy] in Russia? Does it know even, dazzled as it is by the lights of its own philosophy, what the Uniates are?[3]

In his *The Icon and the Axe: An Interpretive History of Russian Culture*, James H. Billington recounted how,

> The Catholic Church attracted many Russian aristocrats—particularly after the official anti-Catholicism that accompanied the crushing of the Polish rebellion. The beautiful Ainaida Volkonskaia, a close friend of Alexander I and former maid of honor to the dowager empress, became a leading figure in Catholic charity work in Rome and an apostle of reunification of the Churches and conversion of the Jews. Sophia Swetchine, the daughter of one of Catherine's leading advisors, became a leading benefactress of the Jesuit order in Paris. She set up a chapel and Slavic library and helped induce a young diplomat, Ivan

---

3 M.J. De Journel, SJ, *Une Russe Catholique* (Paris: Desclée De Brouwer, 1953), 92–93.

Gagarin, to join the order. The Decembrist Lunin became a Catholic and the freethinker Pecherin a Redemptorist friar ministering to the poor in Dublin. Most remarkable of all was the conversion of a large part of the Golitsyn family, which had pioneered since the seventeenth century in the secular Westernization of Russia. Dimitri Golitsyn, son of Diderot's main Russian contact, joined the Church and went to Baltimore, Maryland, where he became the first Catholic priest to receive all his orders in the United States. Ordained in 1795, he led a Sulpician mission to western Pennsylvania, administering a vast area stretching from Harrisburg to Erie, Pennsylvania, from a log church near the present town of Loreto.[4]

It was her dear friend, Princess Alexis Golitsyn, who would pray for fifteen years for the conversion of Madame Swetchine: "I would be a very bad friend if I contented myself to desire for Madame Swetchine the goods of this world and to desire for myself the charm I find in her society. No, my God! I would not limit myself to that; I would pray to the Blessed Virgin, her guardian angel, and her patron saint to join me in asking that she be enlightened concerning the true faith. May her talents which up to now have served only to mislead her, now become the instruments of her conversion."[5] Her realization of the futility of skeptical Enlightenment philosophies to satisfy the mystical aspirations of her heart led to an awakening of faith in Russian Orthodoxy. It was only in November 1815 that Madame Swetchine became Catholic after years of study and prayer and having come into contact with that remarkable political thinker, the Count Joseph de Maistre, a man of genius and a fervent Catholic. An accomplished diplomat, he had been appointed Ambassador to St. Petersburg by the King of Sardinia. It is often said that God sends certain souls into this world with such strong traits of family like-

---

4 James H. Billington, *The Icon and the Axe: An Interpretative History of Russian Culture* (New York: Vintage, 1970), 297.
5 Count De Falloux, *Life and Letters of Madame Swetchine* (New York: The Catholic Publication House, 1869), 141.

ness that when they meet one another, they at once recognize one another as kindred souls. When challenged by the powerful intellect of the Count de Maistre to deal with the Catholic claims and their historical justification, it was to history that Madame Swetchine went to resolve the burning questions: Which Church (Orthodox or Catholic) was the true Church? Was the supremacy of St. Peter's successor essential to the structure of the Church? Realizing that she could not remain neutral in the presence of two contradictory and exclusive claims to be the true Church, she went into retreat to read and analyze over six months the twenty-four volumes of the *Ecclesiastical History of Fleury*, paying particular attention to the acts of the Ecumenical Councils and the origin of the schism between the Latin and Greek Churches. The result was her writing a volume that was completed on December 4, 1815. It contained four-hundred-fifty pages of her observations with further marginal annotations. Even before the completion of her labors, the light of Christ had brought her unshakeable conviction that the Catholic Church was indeed the true Church of Jesus Christ to which one must adhere. "Happy day!" she wrote on August 31, 1815, "when the darkness of my mind yielded to the fiat lux! Spoken by a celestial voice in the depths of my conscience. . . . I owe to Thee, today, the first moments of happiness I have tasted for many years. . . . I offer Thee my tears and my joy! Deign to enlighten me fully, and inspire me with the desire of living to Thee alone, and with the strength I need to remain steadfast to this resolution. I ask it in the name of Thy Son, Our Lord Jesus Christ. By His Cross and Passion, I hope to obtain it."[6] Her conversion was kept secret for a time, out of consideration for her husband. She was obliged to announce her open profession of her Catholic faith—to the astonishment of St. Petersburg—after a storm of criticism arose against the Jesuits for various Russian aristocrats converting to Catholicism. Despite her own cordial relationship with Czar Alexander II, Madame Swetchine as well as other converts and the Jesuits were all forced to leave Russia by imperial *ukase* (edict). Expelled from the country she so loved, Madame Swetchine would

---

6 Ibid., 389.

later write: "In my misfortune, I will never forget that I am a Russian amidst the French." The same Russian patriot had rejected the fears of Czar Nicholas that "in becoming a Catholic a Russian ceased to be a loyal subject." To his friend, the Viscount de Bonald, in Paris, the Count de Maistre wrote, asking that he and his friends welcome Madame Swetchine, now thirty-four, to Paris: "You never saw more moral worth, more talent, and more erudition united to so much goodness." The Viscount would reply: "She is a friend worthy of you, and has one of the finest minds I ever met, which may be either the effect or the cause of the most excellent qualities with which a mortal was ever endowed."

Among the collected works attributed to Madame Swetchine there is one termed *A Religious Examination* which, whether written by her or another, certainly marks the end of her spiritual journey to the fullness of the Catholic faith. Its conclusion is worth the serious consideration of those separated brethren who ponder the unbroken succession of the Popes on the Chair of Peter:

> I cannot remain indifferent to the Greek or Roman Church, because only one of them can be the Church of Jesus Christ out[side] of which there is no salvation. . . . Of the two Churches, now separated, the one which caused the split is not the true Church; it made the schism and shredded unity, while the other has remained what it was. History proves that it is the Greek Church which separated itself from the Latin Church. . . .There has to be in the Church of Jesus Christ a Chief of divine right, i.e., a See and a Bishop to which Jesus Christ Himself has attached the Primacy; [possessing] a jurisdiction which extends to all the parts of the Church; a See and a Bishop who are the center of Catholic communion. . . . I would hold, then, that the Pope, Bishop of Rome, is that Chief whom Jesus Christ gave to His Church when instituting it.[7]

---

7 Quoted in Jeffrey Bruce Beshoner, *Ivan Sergeevich Gagarin* (Notre Dame, Indiana: University of Notre Dame Press, 2002), 33.

A spiritual emigre from the country she loved, and regarding France as her adopted country, speaking its language with perfection and charm, she was Russian and Catholic to the end. At her salon in Paris, she gathered about her the most distinguished Russians in France as well as the leading men of every European capital who counted it a blessing to be admitted to the company of an extraordinary personality.

Suffering from poor health for many years, she felt deeply the vicissitudes of her beloved Russia, and especially welcomed to her salon and chapel the poor and wretched to whom she gave every comfort and encouragement as well as aid. At the age of seventy-five she departed this world, but her writings remain to testify to a life of dedication to truth and with words of wisdom that continue to enchant souls seeking the love of God.

Chapter II

Count Gregory Petrovitch Schouvalov
(1804–1859)
Priest of the Barnabite Fathers

Gregory Petrovitch Schouvalov was born in St. Petersburg on August 25, 1804, of a noble aristocratic family in the service of the czars.[1] His father was a general in the Imperial Army who fought against Napoleon, and upon the latter's defeat, was placed in charge of conducting Napoleon to his exile on the island of Elba. At the age of eight, Gregory was placed in the college of St. Petersburg conducted by the Jesuits until they were expelled from Russia. On the death of

---

1 Fr. Schouvalov's autobiography: *My Conversion and Vocation* (trans. into English, 1877; London: R. Washbourne, 1877) is indispensable for the study of this holy Barnabite priest. Brief articles are "The Centenary of a Memorable Russian Priest: Father Gregory Schuvaloff" (*Unitas*, Winter 1959; 283–286); and "Literary Notices" on Fr. Gregory Schouvalov's autobiography which appeared in the English *Dublin Review*, January 1875, 140–143; 264–266. Various articles on Le P. Schouvalov (1804–1859) appeared in *L'Union Des Eglises* in 1923.

his father, Gregory was sent to the Pellemberg Institute near Berne in Switzerland, a school where the sons of great families were trained in the code of honor. He was influenced by the widespread agnosticism of the time and experienced the worldly pleasures in his trips to Italy and France. For a brief period, he was even attracted to Protestantism. When Count Schouvalov returned to Russia in 1832, he became a captain in the Hussar Guard and enjoyed the splendors of the imperial court. He married Sophie Salitkov, the daughter of one of Moscow's leading families. She would bear him three children. Some years before her death, the countess desired to be a Catholic but had deferred her formal adherence in the hope that her husband would join her. She died after a protracted illness, a Catholic at heart, offering her life as a victim for her beloved husband's return to the true Church. He would never forget the fervor in her voice: "You will become a Catholic, will you not?...Promise me." Shaken by his loss and repenting of his past, Count Gregory engaged in the study of the Gospel and turned to the Orthodox Church for spiritual support and consolation: "For a time, I thought the Greek Church possessed the truth, and, once I had decided to become a Christian, I sought most earnestly, and with a sincere desire, to belong to that Church in which I was born." He suppressed any feelings of attraction to the Catholic Church that may have been stimulated by his wife's example, but became troubled by the subjection of Russian Church to the State and by the divisions among Christians. When in Paris, during the Lent of 1842, he attended the Lenten sermons of the great preacher, Fr. Francis Xavier de Ravignan, and formed a friendship with him and other members of Madame Swetchine's famous salon. He had known Madame Swetchine from infancy: "She had been my mother's most intimate friend, and in her, at the time of my conversion, I found a counselor of high intelligence and of a heart whose treasures she too carefully concealed. All the praise I could speak of that accomplished woman would be superfluous; eloquent voices have told of her virtues. But I cannot omit my testimony to her affection." On January 6, 1843, after a deep study of the Catholic faith, he was received into the Catholic Church at the Convent des Oiseaux in Paris, making his profession of faith in the presence of two dear friends, Prince

Theodore Golitsyn and Madame Swetchine. His conversations with Prince Golitsyn would profoundly influence him: "Certainly, my soul was prepared for conversion, but it was Golitsyn who first convinced my reason."

Count Schouvalov continued to serve Czar Nicholas I in various assignments but deciding to devote his whole life to the service of God and His Church, he requested entrance to the religious life at the Barnabite Novitiate in Monza, Italy. It was during his Barnabite novitiate that he discovered his vocation to pray and work for "the return of that great and generous nation [Russia] to religious unity." There he was also surrounded by kindred souls eager to pray and work for the Russian people to enjoy the benefits of Catholic Unity. He was ordained to the priesthood in Milan on September 18, 1857, a few days after the death of Madame Swetchine, and then assigned to the Barnabite house in Paris. Before leaving for his new post, he was received in audience by Blessed Pope Pius IX, who made a singular request of him, that he consecrate his life for the cause of Christian unity. "Most Holy Father," he replied, "I am ready for this moment on, to make of my life a sacrifice for the conversion of my compatriots." "It is well," the Pope answered, "It is well. Repeat this avowal three times daily before the crucifix . . . and your desires will be fulfilled." Fr. Schouvalov kept this devout practice before the Blessed Sacrament for the two years of his priesthood. Falling ill at the beginning of 1859, he never ceased to call upon all those he ministered to in sermons and apostolic works to "Pray for Russia."

Fr. Schouvalov's book *My Conversion and Vocation* is one of the most interesting spiritual autobiographies of the 19th century and deserves to be better known. "The history of a man's moral life can only be the account of his soul's relations with God," he wrote. As his anonymous English translator noted: "Father Schouvaloff was no ordinary man . . . . Over the frivolous, frail life of his earlier years, his confessions display no glossing. With unsparing severity, he unveils his inmost self, the workings of his unsanctified nature, his terrible heart-struggles, his waverings, his fits of hope and despair, and finally his close embrace of the Savior, Whom thereafter he loved and served so well." Heroic was his intense missionary spirit and his incessant longing for the enlightenment of his countrymen regarding the Catholic Church.

His account of eventual acceptance of the Catholic Faith is a fascinating one for its consideration of issues he had to confront in his spiritual journey:

> Catholic teaching is so logical and consequential; its practice is so beneficent and consolatory; it is, in a word, so sure a guide to virtue, that I cannot conceive how anyone can hesitate to embrace it, who is really bent on being virtuous. And this, I do not fear to tell Thee, my God, Who knowest my inmost heart; I was, in some sort, a Catholic before I was altogether a Christian. Nor is this a paradox; for I still had doubts about the fundamental verities of Christianity when I had ceased to have any as to the authority of Catholicism. Admit, for a moment, said I to myself, the truth of the Gospel, and there is then but one Christian religion, and assuredly it is the Catholic. I could conceive deism, materialism, and skepticism, inconsequential and absurd as they are; but I did not understand how anyone could remain Protestant or Greek, for I saw that authority and unity, the indispensable conditions of truth, belong only to the Universal Church. In fact, Lord, Thou saidst, *'My Church,'* and not My churches. Besides, the Church is to be the keeper of truth; and the truth is one; one only can the Church then be. If all churches taught the same thing under one and the same head, as in the first days of Christianity, they would all be divine, they would all be one, as still are all the particular churches composing the Catholic Church, like members of one and the same body. In such a case there would be *unity*; but as their teachings are different, even antagonistic, it is evident all but one must be false. Protestants pretend that in order to belong to Thy Church, it suffices to believe in Thee, Lord Jesus Christ; but they forget that to believe in Thee is to believe

Thy holy Gospel, in Thy holy Word; they forget that to Saint Peter Thou didst confide Thy flock, and that to be of the same fold it is necessary to have the same shepherd. As to the authority they deny, hast Thou not established it by these words: 'And if he will not hear them, tell the Church. And if he will not hear the Church, let him be to thee as the heathen and the publican' (Matt. 18: 17). Thou hast given an authority to Thy Church, having ordained that we should not make our complaints to Thee, but to Thy Church. Thou recognizest a visible Church, to which complaint is to be made, which is to judge, that is, which has authority. And if there be but one Church, can it be any other than the Catholic? Is not Catholicity one of the characteristics of truth, as are unity and authority? Thy Church, moreover, is the only one that believes in its own authority, and that dares to proclaim it. And now, where and in whom does this authority reside? For evidently it must reside somewhere: then it must have a visible head. The only society believing this truth, the only one putting it in practice is, I have said, the Catholic Church; the only one, too, independent of temporal power in all that concerns its jurisdiction for the interests of souls. All other Christian societies are subject to the yoke of a prince; the Catholic Church alone has a head who can say to such a Bishop, prince, or people: 'You are not in the truth, you are no longer part of the Church.'

[As to the Russian Church], a few unlearned persons regard it as the rival of the Catholic Church. Where is her authority? In the hands of a Bishop, of a synod, or of a patriarch? . . . but who among my fellow countrymen would not be obliged to confess that, separated from unity, she has been necessarily absorbed by the secular power? In fact, let a Bishop of the Russian Church fall into any new heresy, and carry his diocese along with him, who will reclaim him or condemn him? Who will maintain unity of dogma? [Prince Ivan Gagarin and I] read a Russian work by M. Mouraviev, *The Truth about the Universal Church*, and its object was to prove that the Greek Church was the Universal Church. Happily for us, and for every impartial reader, this book fails in is purpose; for it proves in fact the truth, while seeking to defend error; and after studying it with care, we were almost thoroughly convinced that the Church which calls itself Catholic is the only one which in fact is so. A name may be usurped, but none can force the public to give it where it does not apply: Titles have value only where they are legitimate. . . . The separated Greek Church believes in the necessity of authority and the unity of a visible Church, but both these are wanting to it. . . . The great step to be taken [by our Russian people] is to recognize Unity and Authority; that authority . . . which still sits in St. Peter's at Rome. . . . As to our Russian Synod, I put it to the good faith of my fellow countrymen, is there but one among them who is a believer in its authority, in its infallibility? No, assuredly. Can it be demanded that an intelligent being should submit to an authority that is liable to err? Infallibility is the necessary condition of our being sure, of our having certainty, of faith. Now this infallibility is possessed and believed in only by the Catholic Church.[2]

The "Association Schouvalov"

The great cause of Fr. Schouvalov's life was the restoration of the Greco-Russian Churches to Catholic Unity, to "true orthodoxy." The Russian prince who would die in the Barnabite habit sought to establish an apostolic group in Paris to gather people together to pray for this holy intention. It was to be realized in concrete form by his fellow Barnabite, Fr. Caesar Tondini de'Quarenghi.[3] Three years after Schouvalov's death, Fr. Tondini distinctly heard a voice (which he recognized as that of Fr. Schouvalov) saying: "What Fr.

---

2 Fr. Schouvalov in *My Conversion and Vocation* (London: R. Washbourne, 1877), 175–177; 184; 198–199.
3 Ibid., 307–311.

Spencer has done for England, must also be done for Russia." This was a reference to the convert from the Church of England, Fr. Ignatius Spencer, organizing an association for prayer for the return of England to the Catholic Church. Thus, with great energy, Fr. Tondini established in 1862 an "Association of Prayer for the Triumph of the Immaculate Blessed Virgin" to encourage prayers for the conversion of the Greco-Russian peoples. Later, it was known as the "Association of Prayers in honor of Mary Immaculate for the Return of the Greco-Russian Church to Catholic Unity." Pius IX issued some briefs blessing its formation, and in 1877, Pope Leo XIII, at the request of Cardinal Billio, a Barnabite, extended the scope of its prayer as "The Association for the Return to Rome of all Christians Separated from the Holy See," gracing it with a number of indulgences. For the years of its existence, it was popularly known as the "Association Schouvalov" with Fr. Tondini as its indefatigable propagator, writing a large number of books, pamphlets, and tracts dealing with the reunion of the Eastern Churches. In a remarkable series of initiatives, he obtained for the association the warm approval of Bishops in France, England, Belgium, Germany, and Ireland.

Today, there are various prayer groups that pray and work for the Unity of Christians, but there appears to be lacking among them the precise focus of Fr. Schouvalov's Association of Prayers that prayer and Masses and works of charity be offered specifically for the conversion of Russia and return of the other separated Eastern to the visible unity of the Catholic Church. Hopefully, such an association may be revived among Catholics with the use of such beautiful prayers as the following entirely composed of texts taken from the Greek-Slavonic Liturgy:

> Full of confidence in thee, O Mother of God and Ever-Virgin, together with our separated brethren we honour in thy Conception the foundation of salvation, the basis of grace and the stay of our hope. Listen favourably, O Mary, to the prayer which we offer up to thee for these our brethren who with us, address thee as 'All holy, Arbiter of the gifts of God' and 'Her by whom we obtain all good.' Grant

that, acknowledging at last, the divine authority of that Peter, whom they themselves designate 'the foundation of the Church, supreme foundation of the Apostles, Bearer of the Keys of the Kingdom of Heaven, indestructible basis of dogmas,' they may soon return to the obedience of the Roman Pontiff, whom, in the person of the great St. Leo, they call 'their own Pastor, Inheritor of the throne and Primacy of Peter, and Head of the Church.' Amen.[4]

In 1917, the All-holy Mother of God appeared in Fatima requesting prayers for the conversion of sinners and, in particular, for the conversion of Russia. In that stupendous private revelation was disclosed the mysterious designs of God regarding a mystical relationship between Russia and the Immaculate Heart of Mary and the Papacy. Father Schouvalov who offered his life for the work of a Catholic Russia often referred to the ancient Latin refrain to Our Lady so often repeated by the Popes—*Tu sola in universo mundo cunctas haereses intermisti* (Thou alone in the entire world has crushed all the heresies). For him, there was no question that reunion would result from the intercession of the Mother of God:

> Yes, they will return. It is not in vain that they have preserved among the treasures of the faith the cultus of Mary; it is not in vain that they invoke her, that they believe in her Immaculate Conception, perhaps without realizing it and without the joyful [formal] commemoration of it.... Yes, Mary is the bond which will unite the two Churches, and make of all who love her one people, one brotherhood under the paternity of the Vicar of Jesus Christ.[5]

In the Third Secret of Fatima, the Mother of God prophesied the suffering and martyrdom of countless Catholics and Orthodox who would give their lives for Christ in the ruthless persecutions and wars of the 20th century, especially those under the Communists who oppressed the peoples behind the Iron Curtain. In the blood of such

---

4 Ibid., 326–327.
5 Ibid., 86–87.

martyrs, there has resulted the longing for visible unity among all those who honor the All-holy Mother of God. In 1858, some sixteen years after becoming Catholic, Fr. Schouvalov exclaimed: "And how should I not esteem myself happy. . . . We are the first-fruits of that Union which every Christian must desire, and which will be accomplished. Do not fear; our sorrows and our prayers will find favour before God—Russia will be Catholic."[6]

Among the 19th century pioneers of Unity between Catholics and Orthodox stand out the saintly Barnabite priest Fr. Gregory Schouvalov and his devoted confrere Fr. Caesar Tondini who prepared the way for the Orthodox to have a better understanding of the Petrine Primacy in the Church.

---

6 Ibid., 221.

Chapter III
Ivan Sergievich Gagarin, SJ (1814–1882)

Prince Ivan Sergievich Gagarin was born in Moscow on July 20, 1814, of a noble aristocratic family.[1] His father, Prince Sergey Ivanovich, was an important member of the Council of the Empire and had three daughters, Ivan his only son. His mother was very devout and provided a deeply religious Orthodox home. At the age of six, he was taken to Paris where he began to be exposed to French culture, being introduced by a tutor in French literature and in the Latin and Greek

---

1 Sources: *Ivan Sergeevich Gagarin: The Search for Orthodox and Catholic Union* by Jeffrey Bruce Beshoner, is an excellent study of the Jesuit's unionist activities and his influence on intellectuals of the period. His article "Father Ivan Sergeevich Gagarin, SJ: The Responses of Granovskii, Kireevski, and Chaadaev to the Russian Question" appeared in *Diakonia*, vol. xxix, no. 1 (1996), 49–56;
Helen Iswolsky's *Soul of Russia* (London: Sheed & Ward, 1944), 95–97;
Dennis Linehan, SJ, published the article "Jean-Xavier Gagarin and the Foundation of Etudes" in *Diakonia*, vol. xxi, no. 2 (1987), 89–98;
Prof. David M. Matual published the article "Ivan Gagarin: Russian Jesuit and Defender of the Faith" in *Diakonia*, vol xxiv., no. 1 (1991), 5–18;
I.S. Gagarine–G.Th. Samarine: Correspondance 1838–1842 (Introduction de Francois Rouleau; Preface de Serge Galievsky (Plamia: 2002), 308).

classics. Aristocratic, deeply devoted to his native land, and highly cultured becoming acquainted with such friends as Pushkin, Tjutchjev, Chaadayev, Samarin, Kireevskij, Leskov, and others among the 'iterati,' Prince Gagarin prepared to serve in the Foreign Diplomatic mission and to be active in governmental and intellectual life. He would become influenced by the works of Peter Chaadayev who had argued that Russia needed to borrow the best in European culture and to seek union with the Pope for the Russian Church to be free from State domination and for Russia to become a spiritual center for the rejuvenation of Europe. Chaadayev declared:

> The day on which all the Christian sects will reunite will be the day on which the schismatic churches penitently and humbly decide to acknowledge, in sack and cinders, that by separating from the mother church they rejected the effects of this sublime prayer of the Savior: Holy Father, preserve in thy name those whom thou hast given me, so that they may be one as we are one. Were the Papacy, as they suggest, a human institution—as if things of this stature could be made of human hands—what difference would it make? It is certain that in this time the Papacy resulted essentially from the spirit of Christianity and that today, as a constant visible sign of unity, it is an even greater sign of union [among peoples].[2]

For Prince Gagarin, Chaadayev had shown how the schism with Rome had estranged the Slavs from the life of Christendom and the principles of European civilization. He would write: "I owe the principle of my conversion to Chaadayev."[3] However, in 1835, Gagarin still regarded the Catholic Church as but a human institution, "a great ruin," and regarded "the idea of bringing Catholicism into Russia" an "absurdity."[4] By 1838, however, he had become convinced that the Catholic Church was not only the engine of civilizational

---

2 Jeffrey B. Beshoner, *Ivan Sergeevich Gagarin, SJ: The Search for Orthodox and Catholic Union*, 18–19.
3 Ibid., 19.
4 Ibid., 19.

progress and the only means of "ending despotism and barbarism in Russia" but that Russia had a pre-Schism Catholic heritage which had been sadly rejected.[5] His sympathies for Catholicism were furthered by Chaadayev's "Philosophical Letters" which proceeded to examine the state and vices of Russian society. For his Letters' criticisms of Russian Orthodoxy, Chaadayev was declared officially insane by Czar Nicholas I, subjected to medical treatment, confined to his home, and forbidden publication of his writings.

Writing in 1839 in his *Journal* detailing his impressions of life in Russia, the French nobleman Marquis de Custine gave this account of "the danger one runs in Russia in saying what he thinks of the Greek religion and its lack of moral influence":

> Some years a man of parts [Peter Chaadayev] respected by everyone in Moscow, noble of birth and of character, but, unfortunately for him, devoured by love of truth—a dangerous passion anywhere but fatal in that country—dared to state that the Catholic religion is more conducive to the development of minds, to the progress of the arts than the Byzantine-Russian religion; thus he thought as I do and dared to express himself—an unpardonable crime for a Russian. The life of the Catholic priest, he said in his book, a life entirely spiritual—or at least it should be—is a voluntary and daily sacrifice of the vulgar tendencies of human nature. This is the proof in action, incessantly renewed on the altar of faith to prove to impious eyes that man is not entirely subjected to physical force, and that he can receive from a superior power the means of escaping the laws of the material world. Then he adds: 'Thanks to the reforms effected by time, the Catholic religion can no longer use its virility except to do good.' In short, he maintained that the Slav race had need of Catholicism to achieve its great destiny because in this religion are found, at the same time, sustained enthusiasm, endlessly renewed devotion, perfect charity, and pure discernment. He supported his opinion

---

5   Ibid., 20.

with a large number of proofs and forced himself to show the advantages of an independent religion, that is to say a universal religion, over local religions—religions limited by policy; in brief, he professed a belief that I have never ceased to defend with all my strength.

This book, which escaped the attention of the censors—I do not know by what miracle or by what subterfuge—set Russia on fire. Petersburg and holy Moscow cried out with rage and alarm; at last the conscience of the faithful was so disturbed that from one end of the Empire to the other punishment for this imprudent advocate of the Mother of the Christian Churches was demanded; in the end there was not enough knout, not enough Siberia, not enough galleys, not enough mines, not enough fortresses, not enough solitudes in all the Russias to reassure Moscow and its Byzantine Orthodoxy against the ambition of Rome served by the impious doctrine of this man, traitor to God and to his country!

The sentence which would decide the fate of such a great criminal was awaited with anxiety; this sentence was slow in coming and people had already despaired of the supreme penalty when the Emperor, in his merciful impassiveness, declared that the man was not a criminal to be punished but a madman to be locked up: he added that the sick man would be turned over to the care of doctors.

This new form of torture was applied without delay and in a fashion so severe that the supposed fool was near justifying the derisory sentence of the absolute chief of the Church and of the State. This martyr of the truth was on the verge of losing the sanity which was denied him by a decision from on high. Today, at the end of three years of a treatment rigorously observed, a treatment as degrading as it was cruel, the unfortunate theologian of broad horizons, only begins to enjoy a little liberty. But is this not a miracle! Now he doubts his own sanity and, on the faith of the imperial word, he declares himself insane.

This is a very recent example of the way affairs of conscience are treated in Russia today.[6]

While in Paris, as the third secretary to the Russian ambassador, Prince Gagarin frequented Madame Swetchine's famed salon, became her friend, and there met leading French and Russian intellectuals who sparked in him an interest in the theological questions separating Rome and Russian Orthodoxy. Madame Swetchine had been strikingly described by the literary critic Charles Saint-Beuve as *"the older sister of de Maistre and the younger sister of Saint Augustine."*[7] Gagarin would add his own later tribute:

> That which touched me most in her, was the passionate love, the unswerving devotion to truth; one sensed, one saw that she could experience a true joy in the search, in the contemplation, in the possession of truth; this was her life. . . . She knew well that the Catholic faith alone could give the truth in its integrity; but she knew also that particles, bits, reflections of truth are found everywhere. She marvelously uncovered truth amidst the errors which surrounded it; she freed it, she showed all its brightness, she radiated everything which surrounded it. It is God himself that she saw in truth; also she accepted it with love, with respect, without stopping the hand which presented it to her. She rejoiced to find on the lips or on the pen of an adversary, a man who did not divide his beliefs and opinions. She did not look to be right; she did not pretend to triumph over any party; she only wished the truth.[8]

Other noted individuals who frequented Madame Swetchine's salon and who played a role in Gagarin's becoming a Catholic were the Jesuit preacher, Francis-Xavier de Ravignan, and the Russian nobleman, Count Gregory Schouvalov, who described Gagarin as "a missionary

---

6 Marquis De Custine in his The Russian Journals of the Marquis De Custine (Chicago: Henry Regnery Company, 1951), 370–372.
7 Beshoner, op.cit., 32.
8 Ibid., 32–33.

soul wandering as one lost and consuming itself." Like many other Russian nobility of the time, Gagarin was not a believing Russian Orthodox but rather a lax deist whose interest in religion was aroused by his concern for Russia's future and his contact with Catholic intellectuals. Together, Schouvalov and Gagarin read Catholic and Orthodox apologetical works which convinced both that Catholic teaching on the Roman Primacy, the Filioque, and purgatory were justified in Scripture and Tradition, and that the Orthodox often elevated legitimate liturgical differences into doctrinal ones. The works of Count Joseph de Maistre also had a great influence on Gagarin's conversion, which took place in 1842: *"Everything concerning Count de Maistre has a claim to my respect and my gratitude, therefore I cannot doubt that in the hands of Divine Providence, his writings were an instrument of my conversion and salvation."*[9] He returned to Russia but kept his conversion secret, fearing persecution by government authorities since conversions to the Catholic Church were forbidden. In April 1840, Czar Nicholas I had issued an *ukase* announcing harsh punishments for those abandoning Russian Orthodoxy such as the confiscation of the convict's property, ensuring that the children of such apostates remain Orthodox, prohibiting the employment of any Orthodox serf, and ordering permanent exile for "Orthodox apostates."

Gagarin's becoming a Catholic was a gradual process as he searched for religious truth. Finally convinced of the truth of the Catholic Church, Gagarin gave up a promising diplomatic career in the service of Czar Nicholas I to become a Catholic at the age of twenty-nine. As biographer Jeffrey Bruce Beshoner noted, *"This decision did not come easily for him; he began with a belief in the superiority of Western civilization, then identified Western civilization with the Roman Catholic Church, and accepted Roman Catholic theology as the divine truth. Only then could he accept conversion."*[10] From 1838–1842, Gagarin had engaged in a correspondence with his childhood friend Georges Samarine that dealt with the political and cultural conflict between Slavophile nationalists and Westerners sympathetic to Catholicism.

---

9   Ibid., 34.
10 Ibid., 37.

This correspondence led to a consideration of the dogmatic issues between the Catholic Church and Byzantine Greco-Russian Orthodoxy that were highlighted by the Russian Orthodox Procurator of the Holy Synod and imperial functionary overseeing the Russian Church, Andre Nikolayevich Mouraviev (1806–1874). In his Russian work *The Truth on the Universal Church, on Rome and the Other Patriarchal Sees*, Mouraviev especially attacked Catholic teaching on the Papacy and the Filioque. In a letter of February 26, 1842, to Samarine, Gagarin refuted Mouraviev's view of the Primacy of Peter. Shortly afterward on Easter Monday, April 14, 1842, he was formally reconciled to the Catholic Church by Fr. de Ravignan, Lacordaire's successor for the famous Notre Dame sermons.

The following interesting passage is part of his response to Mouraviev's standard charge repeated by so many Orthodox polemicists concerning Catholic "doctrinal novelties" considered contrary to Tradition and of which Papal Primacy was considered the most egregious:

> The Church in different periods had defined the dogmas of faith, but it does not follow that it has added new dogmas which did not exist before. They have always existed, but they simply had not yet been defined. The Faith is not the arithmetical accumulation of a certain number of truths. The truth brought on earth by Jesus Christ, preached and safeguarded by the Church he founded, is something unique and autonomous. It cannot be added to or diminished. But it exists in the midst of this world which wallows in falsehood, and its lies are always directed against the truth. Each time an erroneous doctrine appears, the Church declares it erroneous, and so to speak, marks the boundary between Truth and Error. The truth is one, but error is innumerable. With each attack by error and effort to obscure the truth, the Church proceeds to examine the new doctrine, compares it with the treasure of divine truth confided to its vigilant care, and defines what is the truth or falsity in a particular proposition. What the error

denies, the Church responds in affirming the truth. The entire history of heresies provides a clear proof of what I say. The doctrine of Arius was not positively condemned by the Church before Arius, but even before Arius or anyone else who thought to preach this heresy, it was already considered contrary to the doctrine of the Church. Thus, it is that the truth remains one and unique though there is constant development but only from an external point of view. One can prove that in such and such a century a particular dogma had not yet developed or been defined, but he cannot prove that it was erroneous. Conversely, one cannot say that such or such a dogma once defined by the Church can cease one day to be true.

After these preliminary remarks, let us consider what the author [Mr. Mouraviev] affirms in what concerns the Primacy of the Apostle Peter and the particular promises made to him by Jesus Christ. But here I run afoul of a difficulty that is not negligible, though I do not know what Mr. Mouraviev seeks to demonstrate. He recognizes a certain Primacy possessed by the Apostle while at the same time he strives to contest it, yet nowhere clearly expressing his thought. From some of his words, I gather that he acknowledges Peter's Primacy, but that he excludes from the Apostle a Primacy of power. I do not know in what sense Mr. Mouraviev understands the meaning of "power," but I do know that the Catholic Church proves that it is a Primacy of authority and power that was given to St. Peter and not to the other Apostles. This idea of Primacy was inextricably joined to that of power and the idea of confirming others in the solidity of the faith.[11]

Gagarin went on to defend the proper understanding of Matthew 16:18 as affirming the person of Peter to be the Rock-foundation of the Church. He noted his opponent's misinterpretation of texts from

---

11 See Gagarin's Letter to Samarine (February 1842) (in Correspondence entre I.S. Gagarin et G.Th. Samarine (1838–1842), 308.

St. John Chrysostom and St. Augustine which seemed to deny this: *"If Mr. Mouraviev had paid attention to the clear and profound sense of St. Augustine's words concerning Peter's Primacy and to the teaching of the Catholic Church on the power of Peter and his successors, the power of the Bishop of Rome would have ceased to appear to him as monstrous, and he would have grasped the divine harmony of the Church's hierarchical organization."*[12] In later works such as *"The Primacy of Saint Peter and the Liturgical Books of the Russian Church"* (1863, in French), he defended vigorously the Primacy of Peter and the Bishops of Rome. Many of his writings were devoted to defending the Petrine Primacy since that was the doctrine whose denial lay at the heart of the Byzantine Greco-Russian schism. For Gagarin there was no question of the overwhelming evidence for the Papacy being essential to the structure of the earthly Church. He could not fail to note the lack of a coherent ecclesiology among the Orthodox and their evident need (subliminally felt) for a supreme authority. Gagarin argued: *"You cannot make this pope whom you need, this pope whom you cannot do without. But there is one who is ready made."*[13] In his correspondence, books, and tracts, he responded to such Orthodox polemicists as Alexei Khomiakov, I. Kiereevski, and the ex-Catholic Abbé Rene Guettee on a variety of controversial issues. Not surprisingly, the Russian government did not fail to subsidize financially various writers' attacks on "the traitor Gagarin." The Russian secret police were directed to watch Gagarin's activities in Paris.

Upon his becoming Catholic, Gagarin felt that the great object of his life was to pray and work for the reunion of the Russian and other Slav peoples with the Catholic Church. Believing the support of a missionary order was necessary to accomplish such a holy task, he had sought entrance into the Jesuit order that he admired, and which was in the forefront of the Church's struggles. Now known as Jean-Xavier Gagarin of the Society of Jesus, he would be joined by other Russian converts who would also become Jesuits: Fathers Ivan Matveevich Martynov, Evgenii Petrovich Balabin, and Pavel

---

12   Ibid., 308.
13   David M. Matual, "Ivan Gagarin: Russian Jesuit and Defender of the Faith" (*Diakonia*, vol. xxiv., no. 1 (1991), 14.

Osippvich Balabin, all of whom would later collaborate with his many activities and help establish the famous Bibliotheque Slav, an indispensable library of Slav books and manuscripts.

From 1845–49 in France, Gagarin studied dogmatic theology, and in 1856, wrote a pamphlet in French *"Will Russia be Catholic?"* which created a sensation among Catholics. It also resulted in criticisms by Polish writers hostile to Russian interests and controversies with Russian Orthodox polemicists. It would soon be translated into Russian, Spanish, and German, giving to a larger public his favorite themes: Catholicism was not revolutionary; it was not to be confused with Latin Polonism; and a Catholic Russia would not only extend the Church into Asia and the Far East, into China and India, but would confront Islam. His belief that only the Catholic Church could save Russia from revolution was a prophecy that may be said to have been fulfilled by the Bolshevik Revolution of 1917 and its horrors. That same year, he established the French theological review *Etudes de theologie, de philosophie et d'histoire* (it still appears today as *Etudes*).[14] Its first issues dealt with Russian affairs but later, to his bitter disappointment, was diverted to only occasional coverage of Eastern ecclesiastical matters. His many books and articles were directed at eradicating anti-Catholic prejudices among his countrymen and to promote their reconciliation. He understood only too well that his countrymen had little opportunity to know anything about the Catholic Church in view of a "mass of misunderstandings, prejudices, and false notions which form a thick blindfold over the eyes and keep people from discerning the simplest and clearest things."

In 1871, Gagarin published a book *The Russian Clergy* giving his views on the necessary reforms to improve their education and social status (an English translation was soon made and is still available). In 1876, he published *The Russian Church and the Immaculate Conception* showing that it was not foreign to the Russian Church and was, in fact, defended by the Kiev school of theologians in the Orthodox Ukraine. He founded various prayer groups for the conversion of Russia such as the *Petrusverein* (Circle of St. Peter which existed for a few years

---

14 Dennis Linehan, SJ, "Jean-Xavier Gagarin and the Foundation of Etudes" (*Diakonia*, vol. xxi, no. 2 (1987)), 94–95.

in Germany). Concerning himself with the situation of Christians in the Balkans and Middle East, he encouraged the establishment of schools for their education. Many of his enthusiastic plans and activities were never realized, but if he failed to bring about his cherished plan for the union of the Churches because of the opposition of the Russian government, fervent nationalists, and Slavophiles, he nevertheless left a precious legacy. His polemical writings remain valuable for their defense of Catholic doctrines and their impact on Russia's great philosopher, Vladimir Soloviev, who became acquainted with Gagarin's writings, and himself would enter into union with Rome. Soloviev's views were similar to Gagarin's: Russia was originally in union with Rome; the controverted doctrines of Papal supremacy and the Filioque were never rejected by an Ecumenical Council; the Council of Florence had not been abrogated; and the mass of the Russian people were not really schismatic but only in material error.

A great friend of Soloviev, the renowned Dostoyevsky, who hated the Catholic Church and the Jesuits for "preaching an unchristian religion" had a special animus for Gagarin whom he accused (quite falsely) of "hating the Russian people" and "wished only to obtain rent from landholdings and live in Paris." Gagarin even appears as the character Nikolai Andrvich Pavlishchev in Dostoevsky's *The Idiot*: a Russian "of good birth and fortune, a Court chamberlain . . . who preferred to give up the service and everything else and go over to Roman Catholicism and become a Jesuit, and quite openly, too, almost with a sort of fanaticism. . . . If a Russian is converted to Catholicism, he is sure to become a Jesuit, and a rabid one at that."

A remarkable pioneer of Christian unity with the Christian East who never lost a special love for his own Russian people, Jean-Xavier Gagarin would decry his critics' "blind prejudice" and "inveterate hatred of the Jesuits" which jeopardized the sacred cause of church unity to which he had consecrated his life. During his own search for truth, he wrote: *"Russia does not yet believe that the Papacy is the keystone of Christianity; she does not comprehend the phrase; but already she seems to have a sort of consciousness of its truth, and in her pale there is an increasing number of souls who are penetrated by that truth, and who place their chief hopes in it."* Thanks to God, this is even more true today after the fall of the Iron Curtain. On June 19, 1882, the Russian Jesuit Gagarin died in Paris, his last words echoing those of Pope St. Gregory VII: "I have loved justice and hated iniquity, therefore I die in exile."

Chapter IV
Vladimir Soloviev
"The Russian Newman" (1853–1900)

Vladimir Soloviev, one of the greatest Russian philosophers and an acclaimed spiritual genius, had a profound impact on all those in the 19th century and our own day who are concerned with Christian unity.[1] These include those noble souls whose spiritual journeys to

---

1 Sources: Vladimir Soloviev's *Russia and the Universal Church* (Abridged Version has been published as The Russian Church and the Papacy by Fr. Ray Ryland of Herbert Rees's 1944 English translation (San Diego: Catholic Answers, 2001));
Hans Urs von Balthasar's *The Glory of the Lord*, Vol. III, (San Francisco: Ignatius Press, 1969), 279–353);
James H. Billington, *The Icon and the Axe: An Interpretative History of Russian Culture* (1966), 464–472);
Helen Iswolsky, *Vladimir Soloviev* (The Encyclopedia of Morals, 1956), 552–558;
James Likoudis, "Vladimir Soloviev, 'The Russian Newman', on Christian Politics and Ecumenism" (*The Catholic Social Science Review* 16; 2011), 195–211;
Egbert Munzer, *Soloyyev: Prophet of Russian-Western Unity* (London: Hollis & Carter, 1956);
Aidan Nichols, OP, "Solovyov and the Papacy: A Catholic Evaluation" *Communio*,

the Catholic Church are recounted in this volume. In an article in the *Dublin Review* in 1951, author Leonard Walton gave this description of the famous Russian thinker:

> He was tall and spare. His face with its lofty brow, regular features and sensitive mouth was pale, thin, austere, almost emaciated, enclosed by long locks of slightly curling hair which fell upon his shoulders. But the most striking feature was the melancholy, penetrating gray-blue eyes peering from beneath jet-black brows. *'Such faces,'* wrote the Frenchman de Vogue who met him in Cairo, *'must have inspired the monastic painters of the past who sought a model for Christ of their icons. It was the face of Christ as seen by the Slavic people. It is the face of a dreamer, visionary or prophet—noble, idealistic, full of latent, subdued fires.'* Soloviev was noted for his personal asceticism, goodness, and charity. He would often give beggars whatever money he possessed as well as items of his own clothing to those in need. He was poor, had no home of his own, ate sparsely (mostly vegetables and tea), and had resolved to lead a single life at the age of twenty, living (as the philosopher Rozanov noted) the life of an 'unconsecrated priest.'[2]

Interestingly, he was greatly admired by Pope St. John Paul II, who observed that "philosophy in the Fathers of the Church ends up in theology (as in the case, for example, in modern times) of Vladimir Soloviev."[3] In the Pope's encyclical *Fides et Ratio*, Soloviev was heralded among those "recent thinkers" who established a "fruitful relationship between philosophy and the word of God."[4] For a 2003 conference held in Lviv, Ukraine, on the theme *"Vladimir Soloviev, Russia and the Universal Church,"* the Pope declared:

Spring, 1997), 143–159;

2 Leonard Walton, article in the *Dublin Review*, vol. 225 (1951), 27.
3 Pope St. John Paul II, *Crossing the Threshold of Hope* (New York: Alfred A. Knopf, 1994), 29.
4 Pope St. John Paul II, Encyclical Letter on Commitment to Faith and Reason *Fides et Ratio* (September 14, 1998), no. 73

The unity of the Church was one of the main aspirations of Vladimir Soloviev, who was very familiar with the prayer that Christ addressed to His Father during the Last Supper (cf. John 17: 20–23). Raised in deep Orthodox spirituality from his earliest years, he lived through various cultural periods during which he had the opportunity to become acquainted with Western philosophical thought. Disappointed, however, by the incomplete responses that human reflection offered to the anguish that tormented his heart, in 1872 he returned to the Christian faith of his childhood. His thought, based on God's wisdom and on the spiritual foundations of life, like his insight concerning moral philosophy and the meaning of human history, influenced the rich flourishing of contemporary Russian thought and also made an impact on European culture by fostering a fertile and enriching dialogue concerning the fundamental issues of theology and spirituality. The theme of the Congress clearly mirrors the basic concern of this great author. The study of his thought on the universal nature of Christ's Church will highlight once again the duty of Christian communities of East and West to listen to Christ's desire with regard to the unity of His disciples. Soloviev was convinced that it is only in the Church that humanity will be able to coexist in full solidarity. May the rediscovery of the treasures of his thought foster a better understanding between East and West and, in particular, hasten the progress of all Christians towards full unity in the one fold of Christ (cf. John 10: 16).[5]

The son of the distinguished historian of Russia, Sergei Mikhailovich Soloviev, Vladimir at the age of thirteen became an atheist, but by the age of twenty, had rediscovered Christianity and became a "God-seeker" who would be the great friend and intimate of the novelist Dostoyevsky and even that of the novelist Tolstoy who would reject all organized Christianity. Of a poetic and mystical temperament, and

---

5 L'Osservatore Romano, December 10, 2003.

gifted with remarkable intellectual powers, Soloviev's commitment to historical Christianity reflected his regained belief in God and the supernatural. For Soloviev, "Secular humanism cannot survive on a philosophic base which contends, in effect, that man is a hairless monkey and therefore must lay down his life for his friends."[6] In his rejection of all philosophic naturalism, he would declare: "Not only do I believe in everything supernatural but strictly speaking I believe in nothing else."[7] His ruling passion in the last years of his life was to familiarize his fellow Russians and Slavs with the idea of "Godmanhood," the unity of mankind in a Universal Church centered in the Roman Chair of Peter, Prince of the Apostles. His was the vision of a theocratic Christian society achieving the ideal union of Church and State which would bring about the Social Reign of Christ the King.

Soloviev has been called with some justification "the Russian Newman." Like Blessed John Henry Cardinal Newman, who was led to the Catholic Church from the Anglican State Establishment by a profound study of the 5th century Donatist schism in North Africa, Soloviev was led to a repudiation of the Byzantine Greco-Russian Schism by his study of the historic relations between Rome and Constantinople before the regrettable excommunications of 1054 AD Like Newman, the Russian philosopher took a special delight in the study of Holy Scriptures, the Fathers, Church history, and acknowledged the development of doctrine. Again, like Newman, he had a passionate love for the land of his birth. An acute critic of the Russian and Slav religious scene, Soloviev came to the belief that Russia was in desperate need of the Petrine Primacy to preserve the independence of the Church and to overcome the evils of the exaggerated nationalisms crippling the apostolic and missionary energies of the autocephalous Orthodox Churches. To Soloviev, as Fr. Hans Urs von Balthasar observed:

> The great Schisms, both Eastern and Protestant, are pure scandal; they cannot be justified from a Christian point of

---

6 James H. Billington, *The Icon and the Axe: An Interpretive History of Russian Culture*, 467.
7 Ibid., 465.

view in any way at all. . . . Before the separation of the Churches, the Byzantine Church, out of loveless political envy and the lust for honour, had surrendered to the service of the Emperor and so deprived itself of its Catholic, supranational liberty.[8]

Here Soloviev was essentially repeating what St. Irenaeus in the 3rd century and St. Augustine in the 5th century so urgently insisted upon with regard to the *sin of schism*, namely, that no good results from schism (i.e., formal separation from the hierarchy in communion and with and under Peter's successor). No alleged good can outweigh the immense harm done to the Church and its faithful members as well as the dissenters themselves.

It was in the third phase of his intellectual life as a renowned professor of philosophy (but continually harassed by czarist bureaucrats and censors) that Soloviev was to occupy himself with the tragic results of the Byzantine Schism and Russia's separation from Rome, the center of Catholic unity. This he did in a remarkable series of articles and pamphlets. His masterpiece was *Russia and the Universal Church* (1889), which was published in France due to his constant battle with the censors in czarist Russia who were extreme Slavophiles, i.e., nationalists seeking the union of all Slavs in the Russian Empire and fiercely opposed to any rapprochement with the West, and especially with Catholicism.

As von Balthasar observed: "*Russia and the Universal Church* is a brilliant apologia. . . . In its clarity, verve and subtlety it belongs among the masterpieces of ecclesiology."[9] It was in this remarkable work that Soloviev noted:

> Jesus Christ, in revealing to men the Kingdom of God, which is not of this world, gave them all the necessary means of realizing this Kingdom in the world. Having affirmed in His high-priestly prayer that the final aim of His work was the perfect unity of all, Our Lord desired to pro-

---

8 Hans Urs von Balthasar, *The Glory of the Lord*, Vol. III, 334.
9 Fr. von Balthasar, *The Glory of the Lord*, Vol. III, 279–353.

vide an actual organic basis for this work by founding His visible Church and by giving it a single head in the person of St. Peter as the guarantee of its unity. If there is in the Gospels any delegation of authority, it is this. Jesus Christ gave no sanction or promise whatsoever to any temporal power. He founded only the Church, and He founded it on the monarchical power of Peter: 'Thou art Peter and on this Rock I will build My Church.'[10]

Soloviev struck at the very root of the Caesaropapism afflicting the Eastern Churches whereby civil rulers usurped the ecclesiastical authority of the Pope and Bishops to rule and govern the Church:

The Christian State, therefore, must be dependent upon the Church founded by Christ, and the Church itself is dependent upon the head which Christ has given it. In a word, it is through Peter that the Christian Caesar must share in the kingship of Christ. He can possess no authority apart from him who has received the fullness of all authority; he cannot reign apart from him who holds the keys of the Kingdom. The State, if it is to be Christian, must be subject to the Church of Christ; but if this subjection is to be genuine, the Church must be independent of the State, it must possess a center of unity outside and above the State, it must be in truth the Universal Church.[11]

Though Soloviev's theocratic ideal of Church-State relations would be later regarded as illusory, there is no question of his unshakeable belief in the absolute necessity of the Papacy for maintaining the freedom and independence of the Church from aggressive temporal powers and for preserving the supernatural character of the Church against "the dark powers of the world and of corrupt nature."

It was in this same work that Soloviev uttered his personal profession of Catholic faith from which he never swerved, despite his receiving on his deathbed Holy Communion from a Russian

---

10 Vladimir Soloviev, *The Russian Church and the Papacy* (Abridgement), 92–93.
11 Ibid., 93.

Orthodox priest. This event has been interpreted by various Russian Orthodox writers as constituting a repudiation of Soloviev's "papist" convictions, but it is explained easily enough considering the difficulties in obtaining the services of a Catholic priest of either Latin or Byzantine rite and Soloviev's own subjective conviction that the great Reunion Council of Florence (1439) had never been fully abrogated by the separated Greco-Russian Churches. For Soloviev, the revolt of the Byzantine Greek episcopate headed by Mark of Ephesus and his handpicked successor, the Patriarch Gennadius of Constantinople, and the subsequent defection of the Russian hierarchy, had not annulled the decree of Union declared by the Council of Florence. For Soloviev, the schism existed as a fact, but not juridically. He was aware, too, that any Catholic 'in extremis' could receive the Last Rites from a validly ordained dissident priest if he had no access to a Catholic priest. Then, too, there is the fact that four years before his death, on February 18, 1896, he had been formally received into the Catholic Church by Fr. Nicholas Tolstoy in the chapel of Our Lady of Lourdes in Moscow.

In various Russian works written during the years 1881–1883, he had engaged in a deep study of the religious condition of the Russian people, the causes of the schism with Rome, and the history of the Papacy. His views came to be expressed in *The Power of the Church in Russia; The Schism* (raskol) *in the Russian People and Society;* and especially in his *The Great Dissension and Christian Policy*. This latter work expressing a certain sympathy for Catholic teaching on the Papacy created a storm of controversy in Russia similar to the sensational impact that Newman's famous "Tract 90" had on the state established Church of England. Soloviev wrote—to the discomfort of those ecclesiastics who had substituted Byzantine Greek nationalism for— that brotherhood of love marking the Catholicity of the Church:

> The essence of the conflict between the Eastern and Western Christianity is based, since its origin even to our times, on the question: Is there in the Church of Christ a practical mission to be fulfilled among men? . . . A mission, the achievement of which requires the union of all the

forces of the Christian Church and the arraying of these forces under the leadership of a supreme and central ecclesiastical authority.... The Roman Church alone proclaims the absolute need of this supreme authority, of this unitive principle of all Christian strengths; the Roman Church alone proclaims the right of leading such strengths to the actuation of the practical mission; in a word, to the establishment of God's Kingdom on earth. Hence, the history of the schism cannot be well understood without a preliminary study of the historical importance of the Papacy.[12]

In January 1887, he wrote an article not only accepting the Catholic understanding of the development of doctrine as essential to a living Church but provided philosophical justification for the three dogmas of Filioque, the Immaculate Conception, and Papal infallibility criticized by Orthodox writers. In his pro-unionist writings, he did not spare the Catholics from their share of the blame for the wounds to Christian brotherhood but noted the need to distinguish carefully between the misdeeds of Latin Catholics and the respect due the divine prerogatives of the Holy Roman Church. By 1888, he was convinced that "Russia is not formally and regularly separated from the Catholic Church. It occupies in this respect an abnormal and undecided position, eminently favorable to reunion. The false and anti-Catholic doctrines, taught in our seminaries and theological colleges are not binding upon the Russian Church as a whole, nor do they in any way affect the faith of the people."[13] It was, however, in his masterful *Russia and the Universal Church* (1889) that he systematically addressed the fundamental dogmatic issue between Catholics and Orthodox, namely, the Petrine Primacy of the Pope. He saw all other doctrinal grievances to be "only pretexts, while the Sovereign Pontiff is the enemy." There he summed up his profound religious convictions concerning the Roman Primacy (obtained from his study

---

12 Aurelio Palmieri, "Vladimir Soloviev and His Theories on the Religious Dissension Between the East and the West" (*Catholic University Bulletin*, vol. 20, 1914), 511.

13 Michel D'Herbigny, *Vladimir Soloviev: A Russian Newman 1853–1900* (London: R&T Washbourne, 1918), 29.

of the Schism which inhibited his beloved Russians and Slav brethren from full communion with the Chair of Peter):

> As a member of the true and venerable Eastern or Greco-Russian Orthodox Church which does not speak through an anti-canonical synod nor through the employees of the secular power, but through the utterances of her great Fathers and Doctors. I recognize as supreme judge in matters of religion him who has been recognized by such as St. Irenaeus, St. Dionysius the Great, St. Athanasius the Great, St. John Chrysostom, St. Cyril, St. Flavian, the Blessed Theodoret, St. Maximus the Confessor, St. Theodore of the Studium, St. Ignatius, etc. etc., namely the Apostle Peter, who lives and judges in his successors and who has not heard in vain Our Lord's words: 'Thou art Peter and upon this Rock I will build My Church'; 'Strengthen thy brethren'; 'Feed My sheep, feed My lambs.'. . . O peoples of the world [this means] unshackled and universal Theocracy, the true solidarity of all nations and classes, the application of Christianity to public life, the Christianizing of politics; freedom for all the oppressed, protection for all the weak; social justice and good Christian peace. Open to them therefore, thou Keybearer of Christ, and may the gate of history be for them and for the whole world the gate of the Kingdom of God.[14]

Shortly before his death at the age of forty-seven, and aware of the difficulties and entrenched misunderstandings impeding any immediate realization of his hopes for the reunion of Christians, Soloviev wrote his apocalyptic *The Three Conversations*—which included his fascinating *The Short History of the Antichrist* in which he declared: "I have written it to express my final view of the church problem." In this remarkable work, Soloviev depicts the final union of the Protestant, Orthodox, and Catholic Churches at the end of the world. This occurs with the appearance of the Antichrist during the reign of the

---

14 Vladimir Soloviev, op. cit., Abridgement, 47–48.

anti-pope Apollonius with only a few remaining faithful Christians not having succumbed to the Great Apostasy. These few faithful Christians led by the Protestant Professor Ernst Pauli and the Orthodox Elder John make their submission to Pope Peter II who is hailed as *"Tu es Petrus."*

The Czech historian and philosopher Masaryk would describe Soloviev, the prophetic visionary of Christian unity, as "a secular monk and ascetic," while others noted that he was a "fool for Christ's sake to the end." It is commonly believed that the "third" brother in Dostoyevsky's famous novel *The Brothers Karamzov*, the saintly Alyosha, constitutes a portrait of his friend Soloviev.

Given the profound influence Soloviev's thought continues to have on both Catholics and Orthodox, it was fitting that at Soloviev's grave in Moscow, an unknown admirer placed two icons. One was a Greek icon with the inscription "Christ is Risen from the dead." The other was a Catholic icon of Our Lady of Ostrabrama with the Latin words *In memoria aeterna erit justus* ("The just man will be eternally remembered").

Soloviev's writings had a great influence on several generations of Russian society, including such later Orthodox philosophers and theologians as Sergei Bulgakov, Fr. Pavel Florenski, Fr. George Florovsky, Nicholas Berdaiev, and L. Karavsin. There are Soloviev's Catholic disciples today who work for the restoration of visible unity between the Eastern Orthodox autocephalous Churches and the Catholic Church. There was admittedly a measure of illusion in his thought that the official negative stances of the Russian Orthodox hierarchy did not prevent him and the Russian Church from being regarded as already fully Catholic and that one can profess the totality of Catholic doctrine while continuing to belong to the Russian Orthodox Church. Though adhering mistakenly to the thesis that the Orthodox and Catholic Churches were structurally parts of the One Church, he ever upheld his views on the Papacy as being the Universal Church's divinely instituted center of unity. The Primacy of Peter and his successors was essential to the hierarchical structure of the

Church. In a magnificent passage in his *La Russie et l'Eglise Universelle*, he left this unforgettable and powerful witness to the Papacy:

> The perfect circle of the Universal Church needs one single center, not for her perfection, but for her simple existence. The terrestrial Church, called to embrace the multitude of nations—in order to remain a social reality—must oppose to all national divisions a determined universal power. The terrestrial Church, which must enter into the current of history and be subjected—in her circumstances and exterior relations—to unceasing changes and variations, needs, in order to safeguard her identity, an essentially conservative, and yet active, power, unalterable in its essentials and supple in its forms. Finally, the terrestrial Church, destined to act and stand firm against all the powers of evil in the midst of an infirm humanity, must be provided with an absolutely firm and unbreakable structure, stronger than the gates of hell. Now, as we know, on one hand, Christ had foreseen this necessity of an ecclesiastical monarchy by conferring on one alone the supreme and indivisible power of his Church; and we know, on the other hand, that of all the ecclesiastical powers of the Christian world there is but one sole power that perpetually and invariably maintains its central and universal character and which, at the same time, by an ancient and general tradition, is especially joined to him to whom Christ said: 'Thou art Peter, and on this Rock I will build my Church, and the gates of hell will not prevail against it.' The word of Christ cannot remain without effect in Christian history; the principal phenomenon of this history must have a sufficient cause in the word of God. Let anyone find, therefore, for the word of Christ to Peter, a corresponding effect other than the Chair of Peter, or anyone discover for this Chair a sufficient cause other than the promise made to Peter.[15]

---

15 Ibid., 134–135.

His writings prove him to be one of the most eloquent and vigorous apologists for Russian Catholicism, and he would be followed by other distinguished figures to become Catholics: Princess Elizabeth Volkonskaia, Fr. Alexis Zerchaninov, Blessed Leonid Feodorov, Julia Danzas, Helene Iswolsky, the Baroness Catherine de Hueck Doherty, Irina Posnova, and the great poet, Viacheslav Ivanov—to mention just a few.

Despite the shortcomings of his gnostic and pantheistic leanings, Soloviev's mystical thought concerning the Primacy of Peter and "The Russian Idea," i.e., Russia's having a special mission to bring about the union of the Catholic and Orthodox Churches, and thereby, the universal brotherhood among peoples, continues to fascinate those desirous of fostering the unity of humanity in Christ.

Chapter V
Princess Elizabeth Volkonskaia
(1838–1897)

A major biography of Elizabeth Volkonskaia, a remarkable Russian aristocrat who has been termed "the woman theologian and Church historian who inspired the Russian Catholic movement in the late XIX century," is badly needed. Fr. Paul Mailleux, SJ gave a slight notice of her in his biography of Blessed Leonid Feodorov, the first Exarch for Russian Catholics of the Slavonic rite:

> Throughout the centuries the Russian Orthodox Church has been the national church of Russia. It was unthinkable that the czar would not have been an Orthodox; and if anybody in Russia was, for instance, a Protestant or a Catholic, one could be sure that he was of foreign origin. Nevertheless, during the first part of the nineteenth century some distinguished members of the Russian aristocracy became Catholic. To avoid the difficulties which their change of

religion would have provoked in Russia, they all went abroad and never returned to their native land.

Russian Catholics living outside Russia [Madame Swetchine; Fr. Jean-Francis Gagarin, Fr. Dimitri Golitsyn who became a missionary in Loreto, Pennsylvania; and Elizabeth Golitsyn who became one of the first members of the Religious of the Sacred Heart and was sent to the United States] adopted the Roman rite, that is, the religious customs of the Catholics among whom they found themselves. Only toward the end of the century did some Russians secretly become Catholic in Russia itself, trying to remain faithful not only to their country but to its liturgical traditions as well.

The first of these was Princess Elizabeth Volkonskaia, born in 1838. In her adult life this remarkable woman studied Latin and Greek in order to be able to read the Scriptures and the writings of the Church Fathers in the original. This reading led her into the Catholic Church in 1887. Later, in her estate of the Tambov Government (Province), 260 Miles southeast of Moscow, she wrote in Russian two studies on the Church. In these books she gave the conclusions of her reading and studies, but they had to be printed abroad to avoid governmental censorship. She died in St. Petersburg in 1897, after receiving the last rites from the French Dominican Father Lagrange.

Her daughter Marie and three of her four sons followed her into the Catholic Church. One of them, Prince Alexander Volkonskaia, was a general in the Imperial Russian Army and later became a Catholic priest. He wrote several books on Russian history and the teaching of the Catholic Church....

On the fringes of the Catholics of the Latin rite, who were of foreign origin, a tiny circle of Catholics of authentic Russian extraction were being formed in the capital and several other cities despite the stringent laws against them. In general, they were friends of Princess Elizabeth Volkonskaia and of Vladimir Soloviev. The most active member of the group was Miss Natalie Serguievna Ushakov. Less inclined to contemplation than her good friend, Princess Volkonskaia, she had, on the other hand, a well-developed sense of action and organization.[1]

In 1888 in Berlin appeared the book [On the Church: A Historical Sketch][2] by an unidentified author who was later disclosed to be Elizavetta Grigoryevna Volkonskaia (Princess Elizabeth Volkonskaia). It was published one year before Vladimir Soloviev's masterpiece *Russia and the Universal Church*. She had engaged in correspondence with Soloviev who noted she was "a Russian woman of rare strength and rightness of heart, an amazing energy and a soul that is burning with the desire for truth." Becoming a Catholic in 1887 after a profound study of the issues between the Catholic Church and Russian Orthodoxy, her volume is a forceful defense of her faith and of the Church in communion with the See of Rome. She had become disenchanted with the slavish subjection of the Russian Church to the power of the State and its domination by an intolerant czarist autocracy. Faced with the traditional charges that the Catholic Church had innovated in matter of doctrine and become heretical, she showed at great length that the principle of dogmatic development was a living reality in the life of Christ's Church. It was on the basis of that principle that the so-called "novelties" in doctrine controverted by Orthodox theologians were, in fact, correct expressions of the truths in the "deposit of faith" confided to the Church. She proceeded to show how the Catholic teachings on purgatory, the Immaculate Conception, and the Filioque (the doctrine of the Procession of the Holy Spirit from the Father and—or through—the Son) were examples of a needed clarification and explication of truths rooted in Scripture and Apostolic Tradition. The same was true of Catholic doctrine concerning the Papacy on which she spent the greater part of her book, noting, in addition that a major psychological barrier to the

---

[1] Paul Mailleux, SJ, *Exarch Leonid Feodorov: Bridgebuilder Between Rome and Moscow* (New York: P.J. Kennedy & Sons, 1964), 3–4, 24.
[2] O Tersvki Istoricheskii ocherk.

acceptance of Catholic dogmas lay in the resistance of a more mystical temperament to the "Western predilection for precise definition" resulting from the need to confront the proliferation of errors and heresies troubling the life of the Church:[3]

> To Volskonskaia the Papacy is therefore the core of the question [between Catholics and Orthodox]. All the causes of division between Rome and Constantinople/Moscow are in the end reducible to one: the place of Peter and his successors in the life of the Church. . . . [Her] defense of the Papacy is essentially a reply to three accusations commonly made against it: 1) that the power of the popes grew out of the secular importance of pagan Rome; 2) that the unworthiness of certain popes shows the weakness of Catholic claims; and 3) that the Papal Primacy was unknown in antiquity. The first two are disposed of rather quickly. Volkonskaia reminds us that the ancient Christians regarded pagan Rome as the new Babylon. They were not at all impressed by its worldly splendor or its political and military might. What did impress them was the fact that St. Peter, Prince of the Apostles, had established the Church there and that the Bishops of Rome were his successors. In short, Rome's importance to the Church stems from the Primacy, and not the other way around.[4]

Our Russian author goes on to show Scripture's evidence for the Primacy of Peter among and over the other Apostles and that Peter's successors exercised not a mere Primacy of honor but a real Primacy of universal jurisdiction over the other Churches of the Catholic communion. Moreover, she stressed that the Papal Primacy established by Christ in his Church logically involved the charism of Papal infallibility as defined by the Vatican Council of 1870: "Volkonskaia points out that it is inaccurate to claim that the teaching of Vatican I

---

3 David Matual, "Elizaveta Volkonskaia's *On the Church: A Russian Defense of Catholicism*," (*Faith and Reason*, 1996), 29.
4 Ibid., 42–43.

represents a change in the faith of the Church since the Church has never taught that the Pope is *fallible*."⁵

Though in this work she held little hope that contemporary Greeks and Russians really desired the end of the Schism with Rome, she nevertheless expressed her firm belief, in Prof. David Matual's words, that East and West can be one again:

> Through "the two inseparable pledges of Church reunification": the Eucharistic Sacrifice and the veneration of the Mother of God. Surely, she says, those who offer the great Sacrifice of Love will be inflamed with the desire for a communion of faith and love among themselves. For her part, the Blessed Virgin will gather all her children, in the East and the West, under her one mantle. "The Lord", Volkonskaia concludes, "goes higher than all earthly barriers and deeper than all the divisive boundaries and compels souls to the restoration of unity, reawakening their faith in the 'one, holy, universal, and apostolic Church.'"⁶

Princess Volskonskaia's book was like a bombshell on the Russian church establishment. The Holy Synod thought it necessary to enlist its best theologians Prof. Katanski of the St. Petersburg Theological Academy and Prof. Belyaev of the Kazan Academy to attempt to refute her work *On the Church* that challenged the very foundations of Orthodox resistance to Church Unity. Other volumes of controversy by such luminaries as Professors Lebedev and Sushkov added to the already considerable body of anti-Papal polemic. The result was the publication in Fribourg of an even larger volume by the woman-theologian covering the entire ground of the historical and patristic issues used to support the continued separation of the Churches. This was the five-hundred-eighty-four-page *Ecclesiastical Tradition and Russian Theological Literature*.⁷

---

5 Ibid., 47.
6 Ibid., 51.
7 Tserkovnoe Predanie I Russkaya Bogoslovskaya Literatura. Krititcheskoe sopostavlenie (Po povodu Kritiki na Knigu "O Tserkvi").

In a 1900 issue of the *Dublin Review*, W. H. Kent, OSC examined the contents of this second volume by Princess Volkonskaia in an article "A Russian Champion of the Church," believing it came from a male hand. He noted the similarities of the Russian champion's approach with that of Catholic authors such as Cardinal Newman and Fr. Luke Rivington who had to deal with the same historical and patristic arguments utilized by Anglican writers. Like the Orthodox, these "patristic Protestants" also thought that a recourse to Christian antiquity would demonstrate the falsity of the Papal claims. Princess Volkonskaia met her Orthodox critics on their own grounds showing not only her intimate acquaintance with Russian theological literature and patristic writings, but also her knowledge of the Slavonic Liturgy. She occupied herself in philologically demonstrating that in Matthew 16:18, Christ clearly identified Peter as the Rock on whom He would build His Church, and gave extended treatment to the Fifth and Sixth Ecumenical Councils involving Popes Vigilius and Honorius accused by her critics of heresy and whom she exonerated. There was nothing in their case that implied changes in Catholic doctrine or compromised Papal infallibility. Indeed, she showed that if her critics were correct, their arguments were fatal to the infallibility of Ecumenical Councils and that it was impossible to uphold the infallibility of the Church's Episcopate without belief in the Rock-like orthodoxy and infallibility of the Roman See. Rome was always the real stronghold of true doctrine while Eastern Churches of apostolic origin fell repeatedly into the heresies of Arianism, Nestorianism, Monophysitism, and Monothelitism.

The Dublin Reviewer concluded his study of the author's impressive defense of Catholic doctrine that provided Scriptural and patristic support for the Papacy, observing:

> Undoubtedly, the author's first object was to vindicate the truth in the face of his countrymen, to correct the mistakes and meet the objections which otherwise prove stumbling-blocks in the path of those who were approaching the Catholic fold. For this end, it is admirably adapted, and we trust it may happily bear good fruit among those

Russian readers for whose behoof it was mainly written. . . . [That] the minds of Russian readers are thus directed to the historical and patristic evidence is, in itself, a hopeful sign. After all, the truth will find out its own. . . . May the legacy of this Russian champion of the Church bring forth fruit in the future, and bear its part in hastening on the work of Christian reunion![8]

We are living in an ecumenical age where polemical writings are too easily dismissed as causing unnecessary offense to the sensitivities of our separated brethren, but it is also necessary to be reminded of the dogmatic differences which still unhappily divide us, and which demand resolution. The two apologetical works of Princess Elizabeth Volkonskaia did bear fruit in her day, and they deserve translations to benefit seekers of truth today.

---

8 W.H. Kent, OSC., "A Russian Champion of the Church" (*Dublin Review*, 1900), 117.

Chapter VI

Blessed Leonid Feodorov (1879–1935)

The blessed martyr and confessor Leonid Feodorov was born on November 4, 1879, in St. Petersburg to a Russian Orthodox family of humble origins.[1] His father was a cook, and his grandfather a serf. His mother of Greek origin was highly intelligent, encouraging her son to read widely to become acquainted with the world and its wisdom. Leonid would comment on his adverse self-education at an early age:

> Reading [the Hindu Scriptures] from sutra from sutra, I felt as if I was reading my own thoughts: What is the use of this worthless life? What is the use of activity, agitation,

---

[1] Sources: Cyril Korolevsky, Metropolitan Andrew [Sheptytsky] tr. and edited Serge Keleher (Stauropegion 1993 L'viv); see on Exarch Feodorov, 277–307;
Donald Attwater & Constantin Simon, SJ, "Leonid Feodorov and the Catholic Russians" (*Diakonia*, Vol. xxxii, no. 3, 1999), 181–214;
Paul Mailleux, SJ, "The Catholic Church in Russia and the Exarch Feodorov" (*Religion in Russia*: Cambridge Summer School Lectures, 1939, edited by Count George Bennigsen (London: Burns Oates & Washbourne, 1940)), 31–48.

> generous impulses, effort. Surely the perpetual rest of Nirvana, in which all ambition fades and in which we find the peace of annihilation, is preferable to them. It is better to stay still than to go forward; it is better to sit than to stand; it is better to sleep than to keep awake; the ideal is to annihilate oneself.[2]
>
> ...There was hardly a godless or vicious book that I did not read. I enjoyed French novelists. I was no stranger to the literature and corruption of the Italian Renaissance. I also knew the period of the German *Zerstreuung*. In fact, my head was like a waste-paper basket. We Russians have never known a harmony of faith and life. So I was able to read Paul de Kock, ruminate over Jacoby, and appreciate St. John Chrysostom all at once. But it pleased God to watch over me and deliver me from such chaos.[3]

His secondary studies were made at a gymnasium[4] and an ecclesiastical academy where he would manifest a serious disposition. From the age of fourteen he felt a vocation to the monastic life with his Christian piety developing due to his association with the saintly Orthodox priest, Fr. Constantine Smirnov. After his father's premature death, his mother Mrs. Liubova Dimitrievna Feodorov ran the restaurant which would be the favorite haunt for intellectuals, among whom was the young and brilliant philosopher Vladimir Soloviev. Leonid's intellectual interests, including the study of patristics at the academy, were stimulated by the meetings in his mother's restaurant where he had the opportunity to listen to brilliant discussions by Vladimir Soloviev and question him on the great questions of the day:

---

2 Attwater and Simon, SJ, "Leonid and the Catholic Russians" (*Diakonia*, Vol. xxiii, no. 3, 1999), 187.
3 Paul Mailleux, SJ, *Exarch Leonid Feodorov, Bridgebuilder between Rome and Moscow* (New York: P. J. Kennedy & Sons, 1964), 9.
4 The Gymnasium in the German education system, is the most advanced and highest of the three types of German secondary schools, the others being Hauptschule (lowest) and Realschule (middle)(Source: Wikipedia).

Soloviev invited him to look beyond some of the narrowness of the national Church and helped him to find his place in the universal Christian family by urging him to study the claims of the Roman Church with more objectivity than was customary among his compatriots in those days.

'I was already twenty years old', Leonid wrote some time later, 'when through the reading of the Fathers of the Church and of history, I was able to discover the true Universal Church. Divine grace touched me at the right time, that is to say, at a time when I was losing my faith. A complete reversal took place within me. The Savior, who has shed His blood for humanity, lived once again in my thoughts. I became a confirmed believer, an ardent defender of Christianity, and I decided to devote my life to the defense and expansion of the Church. . . .'[5]

Searching for the truth, he spoke with the sympathetic Polish priest of the main Catholic Church in St. Petersburg. Finally deciding to become a Catholic, he sought to go abroad to do so. As his biographer, Fr. Mailleux, pointed out, "Russian legislation made it practically impossible at that time for any Orthodox to become a Catholic. According to the laws, his property would be confiscated, and the Catholic priest welcoming him into the fold would be deported to Siberia."[6] On June 19, 1902, he left for Italy, and received while traveling in Ukraine a letter of recommendation to Pope Leo XIII from a great apostle of the reunion of the Churches, Metropolitan Andrew Sheptytsky of Lvov. It was in Rome that at the age of twenty-three, on the Feast of St. Ignatius Loyola, July 31, Leonid Feodorov made his profession of Catholic faith. Receiving a private audience with Pope St. Pius X, he was given a special blessing and a grant to make possible his priestly studies in philosophy and theology, which he pursued at Anagni, Italy, and Freiburg, Switzerland. On March 25, 1911, he was ordained to the priesthood in Constantinople in the Byzantine-Slavonic rite by the Bulgarian Catholic Bishop Michael

---

5 Fr. Mailleux, "Exarch Leonid Feodorov," 15.
6 Ibid., 20.

Mirov. Two years later he became a Studite monk at their monastery of Kamenica in Bosnia, and wrote various articles on Church unity, which was to become one of the consuming passions of his life.

There can be no question of the two great loves of his life, love of the Catholic Church and love of Russia. He believed to the end of his life that full unity with the Orthodox was possible without sacrificing or abandoning any of the liturgical, sacramental, and theological patrimony of the Russian tradition which had retained so much of the spiritual ethos of the Eastern Fathers of the Church. The difficulties he encountered were formidable. He found painful the inequality in practice that existed among the various liturgical rites in the Church with some Roman Rite Catholics (contrary to the directives of the Popes) believing their rite to be "the Catholic rite par excellence," even to eventually replace the others. Also, there was in the Russian mentality the fixed conviction that the Catholic Church was "foreign" and hostile to the interests of the Russian people. Catholicism was the "Polish faith." The ordinary Russian simply confounded Polish/ Latin Catholicism with the Catholic Church itself. Then, too, among Catholics of the Roman rite, there remained an acute ignorance of Eastern spiritual culture serving as an impediment to mutual understanding between Catholics and Orthodox.

It was with high hopes that Exarch Leonid Feodorov greeted the formation of a new provisional government under Prince Lvov after the abdication of Czar Nicholas II in 1905 for it abolished all restrictions on freedom of religion. As Fr. Mailleux wrote:

> God knows with what impatience Catholic Russians had waited to be granted this freedom of worship! For fifty years a Russian elite—the Swetchines, Golitsyn, and Martinovs, the Gagarines, the Schouvalovs and many others—had been obliged to go into voluntary exile from the Empire so that they could belong to the Church which they firmly believed to represent Christ's purposes. Others were forced into silence and hiding. They were filled with joy at the thought that they could at last serve God inside

Russia without hindrance and as their consciences directed them.[7]

When the first World War broke out in 1914, Fr. Leonid returned to Russia only to be arrested by the czarist police and taken to Tobolsk, regarded as a spy and Jesuit and in the pay of Ukrainian separatists. He remained there until released by the provisional government in 1917. That same year, at the age of 38, he was appointed by Metropolitan Sheptytsky (who had authority over all Eastern rite Catholics in Russian territory) to be head of the tiny Russian Catholic Church of the Byzantine-Slavonic rite with the title of Exarch. The new Exarch of the few Russian Catholics (it is not known when he was later consecrated a Bishop) realized that his true duty, as affirmed in the directives of the Roman Pontiffs, was to be vigorously faithful to the Byzantine Russian rite and to organize his little flock into a Church that would receive full legitimacy in the minds of his fellow Catholics as well as by the government. For five years he tended his little flock with parishes in St. Petersburg, Moscow, and Saratov. He brought together two hundred of the faithful and ministered to another two hundred who lived in outlying districts of the immense Russian territory. He calculated that about two thousand of his flock had escaped Russian oppression or had died. Fr. Leonid made special efforts to contact and befriend such Orthodox clergy as Fr. Constantine Smirnov who was now the Metropolitan of Kazan, the Metropolitan Benjamin of Petrograd, and even the Patriarch Tikhon of Moscow, who expressed sympathy with the Exarch's hopes for Reunion. The cordial relations established permitted for the first time in Russian history a joint declaration of Catholics and Orthodox prelates against aggressive Bolshevik propaganda, and the holding of joint conferences to counter the spread of atheism. To friendly Orthodox clergy and laity in Petrograd and Moscow requesting clarification of Catholic doctrine on the Roman Primacy, the Exarch carefully explained the nature of the Primacy of the Bishop of Rome. Though he was pleased with the individual conversions that took place (for example, his mother Liubovna, the scholarly Julia Danzas, Dimitri Kuzmine-Karavaiev, Fr.

---

7 Ibid., 36.

Alexis Zerchaninov, Vladimir and Anna Abrikosov, and the nephew of Vladimir Soloviev, Fr. Sergei Soloviev), he was convinced that the Reunion of the Churches could only result from the doctrinal reconciliation of the Orthodox hierarchy. This would indeed become the irenic thrust of the ecumenical directives set forth by the Second Vatican Council. The constant difficulties he encountered in furthering his concept of Reunion from Czarist and Bolshevik governments, his fellow Latin Catholics, and from the more militant anti-Catholic Orthodox viewing him as a deceitful "Jesuit in a riassa [Russian cassock]," were exacerbated by the onslaught in 1922 of Communist persecution and strangulation of the Church. It was forbidden to catechize children; churches were stripped of their sacred furnishings and closed; priests were harassed, arrested, and disappeared. Exarch Leonid was threatened with deportation or to be shot.

In February 1923, after being arrested, the Latin Archbishop, John Cieplak, Exarch Leonid, thirteen priests and one layman underwent "revolutionary justice" at the hands of the vicious anti-religious prosecutor N. V. Krylenko. An eyewitness of the infamous trial, the Irish Catholic journalist and correspondent Captain Francis McCullagh recorded the prosecutor's furious outbursts of anti-religious hatred:

> Your religion, I spit on it., as I do all religion—on Orthodox, Jewish, Muslim and the rest. Yes, as Feodorov, has said, with all the subtlety of a Jesuit, we give civil recognition to football clubs, but we refuse it to the Church. . . .[8]

The Irish journalist also described the noble bearing of the Russian Exarch:

> [He was] the most picturesque figure in the court. A handsome, well-built man in the prime of life, with that strong, gentle, Christlike face which is so often found among Russian peasants, with long, dark hair, a noble beard, and the ample, flowing robes of a Russian ecclesiastic, he formed a striking contrast to the shaven Roman priests with their close-fitting soutanes and close-cropped hair. Although he

---

8 Ibid., 169.

confessed that he was the son of a Petrograd cook, and the grandson of a serf, his manner was as dignified as if he had been born to the purple, and, as we shall soon see, his words were more than worthy of his manner.[9]

The conclusion of the trumped-up trial of its major figures was that Archbishop Cieplak and Msgr. Constantine Budkiewicz were condemned to be shot, and Exarch Leonid Feodorov sentenced to 10 years imprisonment. His biographer, Fr. Mailleux, recounted the sufferings of the blessed martyr[10] and confessor from his stay in Moscow's Butyrka Prison, his being later transported to the port of Kern along the White Sea, and then imprisonment in the labor camps of the Soviet Arctic where his indomitable spirit of faith and charity kept alive the hopes of his fellow captives: Catholics, Orthodox, and even those of unbelievers. Amidst miserable conditions, he reminded his companions, "We are suffering for the schism, and there is no need to keep repeating this. We must carry our cross with patience, for we are a burnt offering without which there can be no spiritual rebirth for Russia."[11] Seriously ill, he was freed thanks to the intervention with Stalin by the wife of the celebrated writer Maxim Gorky. Forbidden to live in key cities and towns in Russia, he was able to find lodging in the town of Viatra at the home of a railroad worker. Exhausted from his many years of forced labor, physical exertions, and weakened by a constant cough, he surrendered his soul to God on March 7, 1935. He was only fifty-five years of age. He was not granted the consolation of having a priest give him Holy Communion in his last moments.

During the farce of his Moscow Trial, Exarch Leonid was termed by Krylenko "a remarkable man" and "straightforward in his dealings; and these dealings should not be explained by simple fanaticism." The Exarch conducted his own defense against the Communist charge of spreading religious superstition among the people

---

9 Ibid., 169.
10 While he technically died of natural causes, the toll that imprisonment and hard labor took on him cut his life short. The Church officially considers him a martyr.
11 Attwater and Simon, SJ, op. cit., 192.

and being a counter-revolutionary intent on overthrowing Soviet laws:

> Feodorov was especially obnoxious because he was so dedicated to the reunion of the Churches. In the eyes of the Communists, he wished to construct a common Christian front against Marxism. 'Here is a man,' exclaimed the public prosecutor Krylenko, 'who has united Catholics and Orthodox in order to conspire against the government!' . . . Every one of his sermons against godlessness is political agitation against the revolution. The appearance of a Russian Catholic priest taking the lead among the Roman Catholic clergy of the Latin rite caused a sensation in Moscow and throughout the land. So did his words: 'Although we obey the Soviet leadership in all sincerity, nevertheless we look on it as a punishment sent by God for our sins.'[12]

At the beginning of his stirring defense, Exarch Leonid Feodorov delivered one of the most impressive testimonies for the Catholic faith and for the truth of the Petrine office of the Bishop of Rome to be publicly professed before believers and unbelievers in Moscow:

> My whole life has been based on two foundations: love of the Church to which I have united myself, and love of my country which is dear to me. I do not mind whether I am condemned to ten years of imprisonment, or to be shot, but this is not because I am a fanatic. Since I gave myself to the Catholic Church, my chief idea has been to reconcile my country with it, because I believe it to be the one true Church. The government has not understood us. . . . If everything we have said in our meetings and our discussions was known, we would not be here, accused of having held secret meetings. That accusation is utterly without foundation. If we opposed the decrees which disposed of Church property without any consideration for the religious consciences of Catholics, it was not at all

---

12 Ibid., 191.

through concern for ourselves, but solely because of the laws of the Church. For us the canons of the Church are absolutely sacred things. The supreme pastoral authority of the Roman Pontiff is a dogma of our Catholic faith, and submission to the man whom we consider to be the representative of Jesus Christ on earth is a strict obligation for us. So it is a question of principle for us, and not of disobeying the law for our own material interests. . . . We are the victims of understanding, and I do not see how we can escape from this. If the Almighty will accept our sacrifice on this Palm Sunday, if some good seed may spring from our bodily suffering, to grow and ripen, to be accepted and appreciated by our dear fatherland which I love so deeply, I wish only that through this experience, however painful it may be, our fatherland may come to realize that the Christian faith and the Catholic Church are not political organizations but a community of love. In this I see the providence of God, the will of God, and believing this I am prepared to accept whatever he sends.[13]

It is to be hoped that an eight-hundred-thirty-three-page book in Russian with many illustrations on the life of Blessed Leonid that was published in 1963 by the Ukrainian confessor Joseph Slipyj (later Cardinal) will be translated into English to complement Fr. Paul Mailleux's fine study. In addition, it would be eminently desirable to see published in English the Blessed's widespread correspondence, two catechisms, and a work that survived the police in Solovki (*Jesus Christ as an Historical Person*). From 1903 to 1918, sixty-eight issues of the magazine *Slovo Istiny* ("The Word of Truth") were published by Russian Catholics in St. Petersburg. They contained some precious articles on Church unity by Blessed Leonid.

Declared a Servant of God in November 1997, he was beatified by Pope St. John Paul II on June 27, 2001. May all readers invoke Blessed Leonid Feodorov for the Unity of all Christians with the prayer he himself composed:

---

13 Mailleux, SJ, op. cit., 171–172, 176.

O Merciful Lord, Our Savior, hear the prayers and petitions of Your unworthy sinful servants who humbly call upon You and make us all to be one in Your one, holy, catholic and apostolic Church. Flood our souls with Your unquenchable light. Put an end to religious disagreements, and grant that we Your disciples and Your beloved children may all worship You with a single heart and voice. Fulfill quickly, O grace-giving Lord, Your promise that there shall be one Divine Shepherd of Your Church; and may we be made worthy to glorify Your Holy Name now and ever and unto the ages of ages. Amen.

Chapter VII
Dr. Irene Posnov[1*] (1914–1997)
Daughter of Mikail Emmanuelovich Posnov
(1873–1931)

An early ecumenist, Jean Rupp, the Bishop of Monaco, who made some important visits to the Soviet Union during the Cold War to speak to Russian churchmen, first drew attention in his *Explorations*

---

1 * Sources: James Likoudis, Little Known Russian Orthodox Historian on the Papacy, (*The Wanderer*, June 23, 2011), 2;

Jean Rupp, Bishop of Monaco, Les Conciles Du Premier Millenaire et l'Eglise Romaine Selon un Auteur Orthodoxe, (Explorations Oecumeniques: Un Eveque revient d'U.R.S.S.(Editions Pastorelly, Monte Carlo 1967);

Jean Rupp, Bishop of Monaco, The Christian Church Until 1054 – A Review Article, (*Journal of Ecumenical Studies*, 1965);

Irene Posnoff, Letter of the 'Foyer Oriental Chretien', (*Christ to the World*, January–February, 1979), 49–60;

Irene Posnoff, Russian Catholics and Ecumenism in the Twentieth Century, Re-Discovering Eastern Christendom: Essays in Commemoration of Dom Bede Winslow, ed. A.H. Armstrong and E.J.B. Fry (London: Darton Longman & Todd, 1963), 135–153.

Oecumeniques to the remarkable book of the Russian Orthodox Church historian Mikhail Emmanuelovich Posnov, *The History of the Christian Church Until the Great Schism of 1054*.[21][3] Dr. Posnov devoted his life to the study of Christian antiquity, occupying the Chair of Church History at the University of St. Vladimir of Kiev until he was forced to flee the Bolshevik Revolution. He then taught at the Theological Academy of Sofia in Bulgaria and at the University of Sofia until his death in October 1931. A shorter version of the book was published in Bulgaria after Posnov's death and later, a fuller version appeared in the original Russian by a publishing house in Belgium run by Posnov's daughter, Irene.[4] Posnov was also the author of a great tome, exhaustive in scope, *The Gnosticism of the Second Century and the Victory of the Christian Church Over It*.

It was in writing his history of the schism between Rome and the Eastern Churches led by Constantinople that Posnov became convinced that in the Early Church the Eastern patriarchs and Bishops had indeed acknowledged the Bishop of Rome's authority and jurisdiction. As Bishop Rupp noted, Posnov had studied in Berlin and was trained in the historical research methods of the celebrated rationalist Adolf von Harnack (famous for his 1885 *History of Dogma*).

Posnov, however, possessed a "judicious spirit" and was a seeker of objective truth. He proceeded to assess in scholarly fashion the history of the seven Ecumenical Councils only to find concrete evidence of Papal supremacy as an indispensable factor in the dogmatic life of the Church. Interestingly, his daughter Irene became a Catholic and the leader of the Russian Catholic community in Belgium.

In his survey of the growth of the Church, its struggle with the early heresies, the key writings of the major apologists and fathers, and aspects of Christian worship and sacramental practice, Dr. Posnov noted that Christians from the beginning believed that

2 [1] Jean Rupp, *Explorations Oecumeniques* (Monte Carlo: Editions Pastorelley, 1967).

3 [2] Mikhail Emmanuelovich Posnov, *The History of the Christian Church Until the Great Schism of 1054*, trans. by Thomas E. Herman, MD, (Bloomington, IN: Author House)

4

Christ founded the Church as a universal institution with a "divinely instituted hierarchy."[53] It is remarkable that though one can still find Protestant and Orthodox writers who scour history to absolutely deny that a real Primacy of supremacy was wielded by the Roman Pontiffs in the First Millennium Church, the Russian Orthodox Posnov had no difficulty in finding the historical evidence that supported the See of Rome's universal authority being exercised in both East and West: "With [its] Primacy of love, the Roman Church was also the leader in the development of Church teaching. All the great questions of Christian teaching of the second and third centuries found their resolution for the entire Church in Rome."[6]

He observed St. Irenaeus declaring that "the Roman Church is the measure for all the other churches. All other true churches must agree with the Roman Church in belief and structure. . . . Only by being in communion with Rome could other true Christian communities exist. And this is not a personal statement only of Irenaeus and Cyprian, but the conviction of the entire ancient Church."[7]

It was especially his study of the first seven Ecumenical Councils that brought conviction to Posnov that "undoubtedly, the Pope did possess [and exercised] canonical authority in the East. . . . The canonical authority of the Pope was firmly established. . . . Many councils, canons, and imperial edicts testify to this fact. With time this [canonical] Primacy had widened to dogmatic Primacy. . . . The history of the ecumenical councils proves that the most important material for conciliar deliberation was that given by the Western Church and the Pope. The material from the Roman Pope, in reality, played the Primacy role at most ecumenical councils."[8] He studied how the patriarchs of Constantinople reacted to the further intervention of the 9th century Popes in the internal affairs of the Byzantine State Church—an intervention intended to safeguard the rights of the Patriarch Ignatius against his opponent Photius: "The Patriarchs of Constantinople realized that with the coronation of Charlemagne

---

5 [3] Posnov, *The History of the Christian Church Until the Great Schism of 1054*, 61.
6 Ibid., 78.
7 Ibid.
8 Ibid., 482.

as Roman Emperor [800 AD], the Popes had become odious political enemies in the eyes of Byzantine emperors."

This attitude prepared the way for the Patriarch Michael Cerularius (famous for his role in the dramatic events of 1054) and his successors to begin "their own fantastic program of self-elevation. The first step in this plan was to be freed from any canonical dependence on the Pope. . . . The Patriarchs therefore preferred a complete break with the Pope, destroying the unity of the Church in order to achieve their independence from the Pope. They preferred independence to unity and communion with the Pope, which only reminded them of their canonical dependence on Rome. They were able to finally end communion with Rome because the Byzantine emperors hated the Popes after the coronation of the Carolingian dynasty. The majority of Greek believers agreed with the break because it had been presented to them as necessary in order to preserve the faith of the Eastern Church from Western errors."[9]

Dr. Posnov also took pains to dismiss what was to become for centuries the chief dogmatic "heresy" attributed to Catholics, namely the doctrine embodied in the Filioque clause that was added to the Creed in the Latin liturgy. In his historical and canonical analysis of the Filioque question, he observed: "No one can deny that in the words of the Eastern Fathers there is an indication of some sort of participation of the Son in the procession of the Holy Spirit." The statements of Orthodox polemicists rejecting the eternal procession from or through the Son "have no authoritative support from the teachings of local or ecumenical councils. Hence, the voices of individual theologians cannot be placed above the general, unanimous teaching of half the universal Church, the Western Church. Moreover, the expression 'Filioque' was not condemned by any ecumenical council as a heretical expression. . . . We also cannot agree that the Filioque is condemned automatically as an addition to the Creed."[10]

Posnov's book is impressive as an Eastern Christian's non-polemical view of the origins of the Byzantine Greco-Slav Schism. It throws much light on the aggressive attempts of the patriarchs of

---
9 Ibid., 483.
10 Ibid., 478.

Constantinople to dominate the other Eastern patriarchs and establish their ecclesiastical hegemony throughout the East with the aid of the Byzantine emperors. Political hostility to the Popes in the West revealed itself early when "the Byzantine emperors frequently were inflamed with anger at the independence of the Popes, especially during the Monothelite and iconoclastic [7th and 8th] centuries."[11]

Emperor Justinian (507–565) especially established the legal relationship of the emperors to the Church and refined the Byzantine union of Church and State, thereby enabling later Byzantine emperors to act often in their capacity as "the sole lawgiver and commander of Church affairs."[12] They would never either forgive or forget the insult to their universal imperial authority when Pope Leo III dared on Christmas morning AD 800 to crown Charlemagne as Emperor in the West. The affairs of the Byzantine Church took an unfortunate turn as its alleged *symphonia* of Church and State "in practice turned into Caesaropapism—the domination of emperors over the Church."[13] One cannot underestimate the eclipse of the Petrine Primacy that took place in the mentality of 12th century churchmen who proved compliant to the political demands of the Byzantine State Church.

He declared "artificial" the theory of five equal patriarchs ruling the Church, contrived by some Byzantine theologians. Posnov stated it had "no justification in apostolic tradition."[14] Despite the tensions between Rome and the Byzantine political-ecclesiastical world which took place before 1054, our Russian historian leaves no doubt that the Pope exercised a canonical and doctrinal authority over the East in the First Millennium Church. It proved tragic when the essentially puerile doctrinal and liturgical grievances given prominence by the Patriarchs Photius (858–867; 878–886) and Michael Cerularius (1043–1058) became inflamed by a growing chauvinistic nationalism among Byzantines which would consider "everything non-byzantine to be heretical."[15]

---

11 Ibid., 218.
12 Ibid., 218.
13 Ibid., 217.
14 Ibid., 247.
15 Ibid., 457.

There are some inaccuracies and shortcomings in this work of a Russian scholar who in his search for truth overcame the anti-Catholic prejudices of his confreres to provide a new and more objective perspective on the historical events that resulted in tragic breaks in communion between Rome and Constantinople. Posnov's work has great value for dispelling traditional Greek and Russian Orthodox objections to the Roman Church's Primacy of universal authority: "The Papacy is an institution not just of the Latin Western Church, but a universal, Catholic institution."[16] The Papacy was not only an indispensable feature of the ancient canonical structure in the Church but as Vatican II would again affirm some 30 years after Posnov's death, the Petrine office of the Pope was not of mere ecclesiastical institution but of explicit divine institution by Christ the Lord. Interestingly, our Russian historian saw no contradiction between the Petrine Primacy and the Easterners' traditional emphasis on conciliarity (or collegiality) in the life of the Church. Both were essential for the Church's effective mission.

Dr. Irene Posnov, D. Es Lettres (Louvain) (1914–1997)

Irene, the daughter of Professor Posnov, was born in Kiev in 1914. Though her father remained Russian Orthodox, Irene became a Russian Catholic, consecrating her life to the service of praying and working for the visible Unity of the Church. From her father she learned not to be resigned to the division between Orthodox and Catholics. She suffered from the sad consequences of the schism separating brethren and determined to spend all her future energies to hasten the reconciliation of the Churches. A refugee with her father in Bulgaria after the Bolshevik Revolution, she did her secondary studies in Sofia where she met the Apostolic Nuncio Giuseppe Roncalli (the future Pope John XXIII). The Nuncio helped obtain for the young Orthodox student a Cardinal Mercier scholarship designed to assist Russians to make their future studies at the University of Louvain. There she earned her doctorate in classical

---

16 Ibid., 486.

philology. It was during her university years that she entered into communion with Rome and would pronounce private and perpetual religious vows. For fifteen years after World War II, she helped Soviet prisoners of war in West European camps and assisted the Russian refugees who had remained in Belgium. In 1945, she founded and directed the Russian Center ("Pro Russia") in Brussels. Its publishing house *La Vie avec Dieu* would print more than 160 books to fill the spiritual vacuum of religious literature for the Russian exiles in the West as well as those behind the Iron Curtain exposed to the onslaught of official Atheism. Aided by her coworkers Fr. Cyril Kozina and Fr. Anthony Ilc and the collaboration of distinguished Orthodox writers, she was encouraged in her ecumenical work by Cardinal Tisserant, prefect of the Congregation for Eastern Churches. As editor of the tri-quarterly letter *Foyer Oriental Chretien*, she sought to acquaint Catholics with the spiritual treasures of the Eastern Churches. In response to the desire of the Russian Catholic Congress held in Rome in 1950, she and her fellow workers also began to publish in Brussels a periodical Russian Catholic review *Russia and the Universal Church,* which was directed at encouraging and strengthening the Russian Catholic diaspora.

Writing in *Re-Discovering Eastern Christendom: Essays in Commemoration of Dom Bede Winslow*, Dr. Posnov marked the importance of a Russian Catholic Congress meeting in Rome in 1950, which expressed its gratitude to Pope Pius XII for defining the Assumption of the Most Holy Virgin.[17] She also noted:

> The principal resolution of this Roman congress was to send a petition to the Holy Father asking for the consecration of Russia to the Most Pure Heart of Mary, as she had desired at Fatima. In 1952, Pope Pius XII replied to this petition by an apostolic letter *Sacro vergento anno*, in which he laid the foundation for a close collaboration between Eastern and Western Christianity in the common fight against militant atheism in the name of the eternal

---

17 Re-Discovering Eastern Christendom: Essays in Commemoration of Dom Bede Winslow (London: Darton Longman & Todd, 1963).

Christian truths. The extraordinary historic significance of this apostolic letter lies especially in the spirit of universal charity in Christ, in its noble witness for the defense of the sacred and inalienable rights of man to liberty, dignity and faith, in its condemnation of the Communist system, in the actual religious act of the consecration of Russia, a non-Catholic, but great Christian country, to the Most Pure Heart of the Mother of God, and in the invitation to safeguard our traditions and to resist manfully the assaults of impiety.

From the ecumenical point of view this letter is important because it shows that the Holy Father recognizes as part of his spiritual flock not only the Catholics but the Christians who are separated through no fault of their own. It declares that these faithful were detached from the Apostolic See by the vicissitudes of history and 'if relations gradually became more difficult, through a whole set of adverse circumstances, up to 1448, yet, since we have no document which declares your church to be separated from the Apostolic See, it can certainly not be blamed upon either the Slav peoples or our predecessors. . . .

Russian Catholics remain deeply grateful to the Sovereign Pontiff for this consecration of their suffering country, which had liked to be called 'The House of Our Lady', to her who had always aided Russia in the gravest hour of her history.[18]

Later, Dr. Posnov wrote that unfortunately she and her fellow Russian Catholics did not know at the time that this consecration had to be done in collegial union with all the Bishops of the Catholic world. She would live to see it done by Pope St. John Paul II on March 25, 1984, always treasuring the letter she received from the surviving seer of the three children who had received the astonishing apparitions at Fatima in 1917. Sr. Lucia wrote Irene:

---

[18] Irene Posnoff, Russian Catholics and Ecumenism in the Twentieth Century, Re-Discovering Eastern Christendom, 152–153.

Our Heavenly Mother loves the Russian people, and I love them also; uniting myself to the secret designs of her Immaculate Heart. I ardently desire their return to the right road which leads to heaven. I know that the Russian people are great, generous, and cultured, that they are capable of walking on the paths of justice, truth, and goodness.

No sooner had I seen the kindness of the Mother of God in their regard than I began to look on them as brothers, and I wish nothing more than their salvation. I know that the true faith, the Christian faith is alive among you; I know that there are chosen souls among you who serve God and sacrifice themselves to obtain the salvation of those who have left Him. Nobody can and nobody must fulfill this great mission better than the very members of your country. It is a task which will take not just one day, but many years of work and prayer. But in the end, the Immaculate Heart of Mary will triumph, and it will be our happiness to have worked a little and suffered for her triumph. Do not cease doing everything you can for the salvation of your people and your homeland.[19]

This brief resume of Irene Posnov's activities on behalf of her compatriots and the Unity of the Church does not do justice to the services this extraordinary woman rendered the Church. Her intelligence (she spoke nine languages), her strong will, and organizational skills were put at the service of a unique ecumenical vocation marked by a true Christian charity for the Orthodox. In 1948, she wrote a small brochure giving her thoughts on what must be done to end the divisions among Christians which contradict the prayer of Christ that all His disciples be one in Him (John 17:11). Among its pages are some striking comments on Infallibility drawn from her wide experience with Russian objections to Catholic doctrine. They retain their great value for ecclesiological discussions with the Orthodox today.

---

19   Letter of Lucia of Fatima to Irene Posnoff (1951), in Bro Michael of the Holy Trinity, The Whole Truth About Fatima (Buffalo, NY: Immaculate Heart Publications, 1986), Vol. III, 308–311.

As one knows, there exists among the Russians numerous prejudices regarding the Supreme Pontiffs. Political conflicts and even 'linguistic misunderstanding' have contributed to create such prejudices. In fact, the word 'Infallibility' does not exist with the Eastern Slavs who translate 'Infallibility' by the word 'Impeccability.' Those who rail against the 'impeccability of the Popes' are numerous and in good faith. They believe that after the Popes had made the Christians of the West admit their impeccability and usurpation of the prerogatives of Holy Church, the Popes then desired to extend their spiritual domination over the Christian East. This is how separated Russians and other Easterners interpret the many appeals in favor of Union that the Popes have addressed to them. When the Orthodox confront Catholics with these questions, rarely do the latter even make known to them the true doctrine of the Church. Excepting a few instances, faithful Catholics do not know that it is necessary to distinguish for our Orthodox brethren the powers of the Pope as Chief Teacher of the Universal Church and those he exercises as Patriarch of the West over one part of the Church, namely, the Latin Church. . . . There is similar ignorance regarding a proper understanding of the teaching of the Vatican Council [I] relative to the infallibility of the Supreme Pontiff. In response to the Orthodox who affirm: 'The Church is infallible,' certain Catholics replied: 'No, it is the Pope who is infallible'—as if the infallibility of the Pope is opposed to the infallibility of the Church!

It is indeed a matter of faith that the Church is infallible. . . . The Vatican Council determined that the Pope does not possess an infallibility separated from the Church; rather his infallibility has been willed by Christ to adorn His Church. Thus understood, the Catholic doctrine of infallibility will be found to be less objectionable to our separated brethren for whom infallibility is essentially the privilege of the entire Church without entering into the question of which members of the Church possess this infallibility. Infallibility pertains in the last analysis to the Church in its totality, and if the body of Bishops in union with the Pope as their Chief possess infallibility, it is because they are the instrument of the Holy Spirit in safeguarding the infallibility of the living faith of the entire Church.

Infallibility has been promised by Christ to the assembly of the College of the Apostles with Peter at its head. The College of Bishops reunited in an ecumenical Council is able to possess the privilege of infallibility only in the measure where it is united to the Pope as its head.... Thus, the infallibility of the Pope is in no wise an infallibility apart, one isolated from the entire Church. In the exercise of his doctrinal authority the Pope is in solidarity with the entire Church. There is a continual interaction between the living faith of the Church as the community of the faithful and the doctrinal magisterium of the Pope. The living faith of the Church is safeguarded by the vigilance of the Pope and Bishops and, conversely, the exercise of the Teaching magisterium is enlightened and nourished by the living faith of the Church.[20]

Adhering firmly to the Russian traditions she loved, Irene Posnov was entirely devoted to her ecumenical vocation, living a rich apostolic life devoted to the conversion of Russia and the triumph of the Immaculate Heart of Mary promised by Our Lady of Fatima. She lived a life of heroic charity, faithful to her private vows of religion in a humble apartment indistinguishable from a monastic cell.

May her memory be eternal.

---

20 Irene Posnoff, Pour s'unir dans le Christ avec nos freres separes de l'Orient (Anvers, Soeurs Missionaires de Notre Dame d'Afrique: Centre de l'action Missionaire, 1948), 36–41.

Chapter VIII
Blessed Vladimir Ghika (1873–1954)
"Prince and Martyr"
From the Romanian Orthodox Church
to the Catholic Faith

Few American Catholics have grasped the importance of the Second Vatican Council's efforts to prepare for the restoration of the Eastern Orthodox Churches to Catholic Unity. On many occasions, the Popes have made it clear that unity with the separated Byzantine Greco-Slavic Churches was among the highest priorities of their Pontificates. Their hopes have been echoed by the many saintly souls across the centuries who sought to heal the wounds of the most formidable schism in Christian history. One of them was the famous Msgr. Vladimir Ghika, born a Romanian prince, who became a Catholic priest and, like many others, died a martyr in a Communist prison camp.[1]

---

1 Sources: Jean Daujat, L'Apotre Du XX Siecle: Monseigneur Ghika (Paris: Nou-

As one of his biographers, Helene Danubia noted in an interview:

> Msgr. Ghika was truly exceptional. . . . He was a great noble figure. I could compare him to St. Francis of Assisi. His poverty, his simplicity, his goodness, his gift of self to all were exceptional qualities, given his noble birth. All that he had he gave away like St. Francis and St. Martin of Tours. He could have lived all his life in royal splendor. He was a real Romanian prince, born in Constantinople of a Phanariot Greek family [phanar: site where the patriarch of Constantinople lives]. His very being reflected his Greek and Romanian ancestry.[2]

Born in Constantinople of a princely family on December 25, 1873, Vladimir was the grandson of the last national sovereign of Moldavia, Gregory Ghika X (1849–1856) and of a family that had given ten reigning princes to the two principalities of Walachia and Moldavia. The young State of Romania was created by the joining of Moldavia and Wallachia and freeing itself from the Ottoman Turkish yoke to become a kingdom. Vladimir was the fifth child of the General-Prince Jan Ghika and Alexandrine Moret of Blaremberg (of French origin). Prince Jan became the Minister of War and Foreign Affairs as well as serving as ambassador at Constantinople, Vienna, Rome, and St. Petersburg. Vladimir received the sacraments of Baptism and Chrismation in the Rumanian Orthodox Church to which his parents were

---

velles Editions Latines, 1930);

Helene Danubia, Prince et Martyr: Monseigneur Vladimir Ghika: l'Apotre du Danube (Paris: Pierre Tequi, 1993);

Helene Danubia, L'Irresistible Amour (Paris: Pierre Tequi, 1995);

Elisabeth of Miribel, La Memoire des Silence, Vladimir Ghika 1873–1954 (Paris: Artem Library Fayard, 1987);

Pierre Hayet, Mgr. Vladimir Ghika, Prince de l'Eglise (La Nef, no. 155, December 2004), 36–37;

Cecile d'Hermitanis, Une Entrevue avec Helene Danubia: De l'orthodoxie a la foi catholique, (L'Homme Nouveau, 16 Janvier 1994), 5;

Louise Gherasim, Blessed Vladimir Ghika–Priest and Martyr (*Christian Order*, November 2013);

2 Cecile d'Hermitanis, Une Entrevue avec Helene Danubia (L'Homme Nouveau, 16 Janvier 1994), 5.

devoted. When his father Prince Jan became ambassador to Paris and died in 1881, Princess Alexandrine sent Vladimir to a school in Toulouse. Since there was no Orthodox parish in the area, his governess took him to a Protestant church, but Vladimir found the coldness of Calvinist worship repugnant. He had Catholic friends at school and wished to take Holy Communion with them. Princess Alexandrine was indignant: "Think of your ancestors! You, the descendant of Greek Orthodox princes wish to become a traitor!"[3] Years later, he would write: *"I waited sixteen years before deciding. The more I waited, the more my soul caught fire. Even at night, this call was within me!"*[4]

After completing his schooling in Paris, he became ill with *angina pectoris* in 1895 and was obliged to give up a promising career as a diplomat. In 1898 he joined his brother Demeter who had been named ambassador to Rome. There he would spend six years, *"a time when the Catholic faith took hold of my mind and heart."*[5] He became convinced that Christian unity was not possible without adherence to the successor of Peter, the Rock of the Church on which the Church was built. It was the Holy Spirit who supported the organic structure and harmony of Christ's One Church, and this episcopal structure of the Church included, by its very nature, the Papacy.

On April 13, 1902, he was received into the Catholic Church by Cardinal Mathieu, the Archbishop of Toulouse who was at the time in Rome. This resulted in denunciations in Romanian newspapers which greatly distressed him. He was termed an "apostate" and guilty of "treason." His mother considered his becoming Catholic a calamity. He meekly accepted such criticism but did not refrain from declaring:

> No, I am not a renegade. I believe in this Catholic Church that my ancestors left without thinking of a split, without thinking of the treasure they were losing. I am going to

---

[3] Helene Danubia, *Prince et Martyr: Monseigneur Vladimir Ghika: Apotre du Danube* (Pierre Tequi, 1993), 25.
[4] Ibid., 42.
[5] Dom Antoine Marie, OSB, Mgr. Ghika (*Spiritual Newsletter*, Abbey of Saint-Joseph de Clairval, Flavigny-sur-ozerain, 3 Novembre, 2001), 2.

> be a Catholic in order to be a better Orthodox. I am a ghost from the Bosphorus and the Danube, a pilgrim from Byzantium to the Mother house of the faith, to eternal Rome. What has attracted me is neither the grandeur of that city nor its renown but the Holy Spirit and the witness of Peter, and the witness of that heavenly Jerusalem before the Lamb of God. A Church cannot be of God that is not the Church that Thou has built on Kephas, on Peter. The tomb of Peter is there in Rome where enlightened souls will be on pilgrimage from the days of St. Peter to the end of the world. Why put an end to a spiritual heritage left by Jesus Himself?[6]

He continued to deepen his faith in God and his spiritual life which would prepare him for his vocation to the priesthood and, much later, his embrace of martyrdom. Because of the fierce opposition of his mother, Vladimir was advised by Pope St. Pius X to delay his decision for the priesthood and to study for the lay apostolate. This he did, earning in 1905 a doctorate in theology at the Angelicum in Rome as well as further studies in Paris to add to his knowledge of Romanian political and religious history. During World War I what was to be a life of heroic charity saw him assisting earthquake victims in Avezzano, Italy, and tuberculosis patients in a Rome hospice. He was not ordained to the priesthood until October 7, 1923, at the age of fifty, after his beloved mother's death. His ordination in the Byzantine rite took place in the church of the Lazarists in Paris in the presence of friends and crowned heads of various European royal families. He had faculties to celebrate the Roman liturgy as well, thus becoming the first bi-ritual Romanian Catholic priest. From 1923 to 1933 he lived in France engaging in intense missionary and charitable work among the poorest and most deprived. He devoted himself to literary and artistic activity, writing spiritual books as well as articles in major Catholic periodicals. His work in the confessional resulted in a reputation for sanctity and this "Apostle of the 20th Century" (the

---

6 Helene Danubia, op.cit., 30–31.

expression of his disciple and friend, the lay theologian Jean Daujat) converted many to the faith including satanists and occultists.

His biographers detail the intellectual and religious influence exerted by Msgr. Ghika in Paris and later in Bucharest. While in Paris, he soon became known among the Catholic elite in that city, which included Paul Claudel, Etienne Gilson, Rene Bazin, Francois Mauriac, Emmanuel Mounier, Charles Du Bos, such celebrated Thomists as Fr. Reginald Garrigou-Lagrange and Jacques Maritain (and Maritain's wife Raissa), and other luminaries including the Russian Orthodox Nicholas Berdaiev. There were many who came to see the holy priest to benefit from his wise counsel. One of them was the remarkable Polish nobleman Alexander Rzewuski (1893–1983) whose mother was a Russian Orthodox aristocrat who had her son baptized in the Russian Orthodox Church. Studying art and painting in Rome and Paris, Alexander would become a well-known portrait painter and illustrator in Paris and immersed himself in its social and artistic world during what he himself termed "the crazy twenties." During this period of spiritual malaise, he was to meet the Catholic philosopher Jacques Maritain who said one day to him quite simply, "I think you should see a priest, and I recommend Msgr. Ghika." This was providential since the Polish-Russian aristocrat Rzewuski had much of the same aristocratic background as the priest. It was to Msgr. Ghika that he would make his first confession as a Catholic, and then proceed to become a distinguished Dominican serving in France and Switzerland.

The princely priest Vladimir Ghika with his slight, frail body, and long white hair and beard, had the appearance of an Eastern monk, a sage and prophet, a veritable icon as seen in the murals of Byzantine churches. As a Catholic he loved Romanian Orthodoxy and always respected it. To an Orthodox monk who asked him why he became Catholic, he simply replied: *"To be more Orthodox!"* He would often repeat this response, as Madame Helene Danubia discovered when Msgr. Ghika played a decisive role in her own reception into the Catholic Church.

I was sixteen when I began my medical studies at the University of Geneva. At that time I had both Swiss and Romanian citizenship papers. Today, I no longer possess Romanian citizenship. I renounced it after I was condemned to ten years in prison by the then-Communist regime. I was accused of espionage for the Vatican and Switzerland. . . . It was at the end of my studies that I found myself confronted by the choice: to become Catholic or to remain Orthodox. I knew Msgr. Ghika was in Paris. Our families were close. We met at the headquarters of the Foreign Missions on the Rue de Bac. He received me as if I were his own child. 'I understand you very well,' he told me. He himself had waited a long time before seeking ordination in order not to distress his mother, Princess Alexandrine. She had actually gone to the Pope to ask him to prevent her son from becoming a priest. He became a priest only after his mother's death.

He proceeded to encourage me: 'Do not fear. Accept your crossing over, even if it means you will be treated as a turncoat. Speak to the good God in your heart. Accept everything. *Be a Catholic in order to be a better Orthodox.*' This saying was his motto.[7]

Madame Danubia made some interesting comments concerning the great obstacles encountered by Eastern Orthodox seeking to become Catholics:

Passing over to Catholicism offends the Orthodox' sense of nationalism. Thus, if you are an Orthodox who becomes a Catholic, you are no longer, say, Russian. I am from a Russian family as Msgr. Ghika was of a Greek family. Thus, you are no longer Greek, you are no longer Romanian, and so on. As soon as you embrace the Catholic religion, you are regarded as having lost in some manner the right to your nationality. You are, in effect, a traitor. The Orthodox do

---

7 Cecile d'Ermitanis, op. cit.

not wish to understand that one can be Catholic and love Romania.... Msgr. Ghika gave his life for the union of the separated to the sheepfold, to Rome. This was the purpose of his own spiritual journey to the Catholic Church. This changed nothing of his love for Romania. If Msgr. Ghika is beatified, it will be as a blessed, a saint, and a Romanian martyr who realized in his own person the union of the Byzantine-rite Churches with Rome.[8]

In 1929, Msgr. Ghika helped organize Eucharistic Congresses. In 1931, he was able to visit Japan, Brazil, and Romania, and when World War II broke out, he was again in Romania to assist refugees and to make contact with Romanian Orthodox clergy, instructing some in Catholicism. When the Soviets invaded Romania in August 1944, there began the terrorism of Ceaușescu's Communist regime and its violent persecution of the Romanian Catholic Church of both rites. The Byzantine Rite Catholic Church was suppressed and forcibly attached to the Romanian Orthodox Church. In 1952, at the age of seventy-nine, Msgr. Ghika was arrested as a Vatican spy and traitor and put in the notorious prison "Uranus" in Bucharest where he was tortured, receiving eighty-three electric shock treatments. Promised his freedom if he would become a "peace priest" and separate himself from Rome, he refused. No one could convince him that the words of Christ, *Thou art Peter and on this Rock, I will build My Church*, were rendered void. No one would be able to efface the words of Christ concretized in the famous words of St. Ambrose, *Ubi Petrus, ibi Ecclesia*. Later he was transferred to the hell-hole of the Fort of Jilava where he suffered numerous beatings, attacks by police dogs, and the freezing cold of 1953–54. Eventually, he would lose his eyesight and hearing as a result of this brutality. To a young fellow prisoner, Teodor Gherasim who survived to write of his friendship with Msgr. Ghika, the priest insisted on sharing his meager portion of bread: "You are young; you have more chances of surviving the Communist hell to tell the world about our ordeals. I know I am going to die here,

---

8 Helene Danubia, *Prince et Martyr: Monseigneur Vladimir Ghika: Apotre du Danube* (Pierre Tequi, 1993), 25.

so my food is not as necessary for sustenance." Nearing death, the holy priest was heard to say, "Nothing is more precious than being jailed for Jesus Christ." Always joyful and an inspiration to his fellow prisoners with and for whom he incessantly prayed the Rosary, he died on May 17, 1954, having offered his sufferings for the Church and his beloved Romania.

The cause for beatification of this "Apostle of the Danube" was begun by the Archdiocese of Bucharest and supported by the Romanian Catholic Bishops of both rites. It was furthered by those who knew, loved, and admired him in *L'Association pour la beatification de Msgr. Vladimir Ghika*.[9]

At the 2012 Synod of Bishops opening the Year of Faith for the Universal Church announced by Pope Benedict XVI, a Romanian Catholic Bishop sadly noted that a recent anti-ecumenical ordinance of the Synod of the Romanian Orthodox Church had forbidden any prayer between Orthodox and Catholic faithful. He added: "We find ourselves forced to beseech God, before our brother delegates, 'Please, Lord, allow at least the Lord's Prayer to unite our children.'" Prayers were lifted to heaven that the Venerable Vladimir Ghika bring about harmony and peace among his beloved Romanian people. In answer to the continued entreaties of the faithful, the martyr of Communist brutality was declared Blessed in a solemn Mass celebrated in Bucharest on August 31, 2013.

Blessed Vladimir Ghika belongs to the "cloud of witnesses" who professed the Catholic unity of the Church, a man of God who foreshadowed the final healing of a disastrous schism so injurious to Christian peoples.

---

9 L'Association pour la beatification de Msgr. Vladimir Ghika (5, Villa Molitor, 75016 Paris, France).

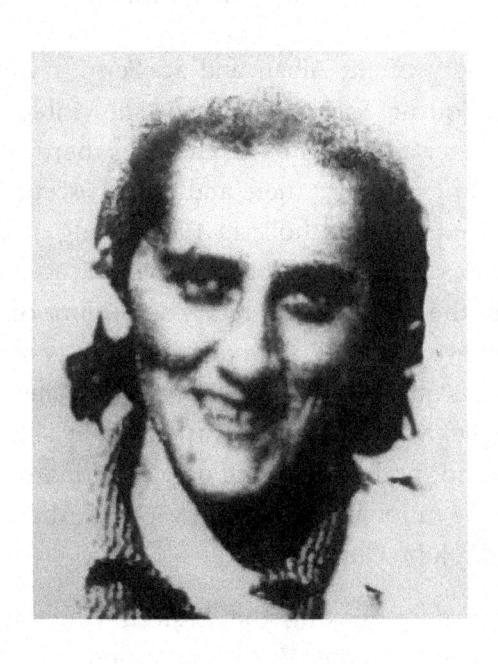

Chapter IX
Helle Elpiniki Georgiadis (1916–1996)

Miss Helle E. Georgiades (known as "Ellie") was born on November 7, 1916, on the Greek island of Syros in the Cyclades. Her father was a twice-decorated captain of cavalry in the Greek army who died in the influenza epidemic after World War I. Her mother came from a distinguished family on the island of Chios. During her young years, Helle became proficient in Greek, French, and English. After her father's death, her mother remarried a banker who relocated the little family in Surrey, England. He arranged that Helle and her sister receive a fine education at school and at London's University College. Helle graduated in physics and took further graduate work in statistical psychology. Five-feet and two-inches tall, she was a dynamic instructor, a born teacher, and began a teaching career in science in various schools. She eventually went to teach physics at St. Michael's North Finchley, a girl's grammar school, and remained there for the rest of her working life. A Greek Orthodox, she became with her closest friend Joan Rutt joint-secretary of the Anglican-Orthodox

Fellowship/Society of St. Alban and St. Sergius which published the ecumenical journal *Sobornost*. In 1950, she visited Rome and the Basilica of St. Peter as well as other churches there. She was deeply impressed by her experience there and by the ascetic figure of Pius XII. After she became a Catholic in 1959 having insisted on being received as an Eastern rite Catholic, she would serve for more than twenty years as the Honorary Secretary and Editor of *"Chrysostom,"* bulletin of the revived St. John Chrysostom Society seeking to make Catholics better acquainted with the Eastern Churches, both Catholic and non-Catholic. Miss Georgiadis was especially skilled in organizing conferences for both ecumenical organizations. In *"Chrysostom,"* she explained the rationale for her work in both the Fellowship and the Society of St. John Chrysostom:

> Our concern in making the Eastern Churches better known and loved in the West is to promote a fuller understanding of the catholicity of the Church and to work for the restoration of deeper fellowship in Christ, so that the unity of the Church can be manifest in the world. It is this *fellowship* of East and West, hindered by centuries of schism and estrangement, which we seek to foster, and which those who have already experienced it in a personal way know will revitalize our vision of the Holy Catholic Church of Christ, and feed the roots of our faith.[1]

In her years of association with leading Catholic and Orthodox ecumenists in England, she was acknowledged as an expert on the Eastern Churches and served as a consultant on Eastern Churches for Britain's National Ecumenical Commission.

Miss Georgiadis was interested in all aspects of the Church's life in England and wrote some important articles and letters drawing on her knowledge of the Eastern tradition to severely criticize the secularist influences which had invaded post-Vatican II liturgy and theology. She excoriated "the false spirit of Vatican II" promoted by dissident European theologians and the disturbing tendency of some

---

1 Joan Rutt, Obituary of Helle Georgiadis, (*Sobornost*, 1997).

episcopal conferences to seek to limit the exercise of Papal authority. She took to task false teaching exalting "the Primacy of conscience" above the Magisterium of the Church and promotion of the ordination of women. It was her special study of the Unity of the Church which led inexorably to her rejection of false theories concerning the Church held by some Protestant ecumenists (such as the Anglican Branch theory). She rejected any "ecumenism" which would accept the idea of a "divided Church," for *"There is one unique Church, and the inviolable aspect of this unicity is the authority of the Church's infallible magisterium. The Church cannot be divided in her authority, because the authority she exercises and which she has received from Christ is the manifestation of the unique will of God."*[2]

As early as 1950 Miss Georgiadis had concluded that:

> The pattern of unity which we associate with the Church of Rome is that of St. Peter, Prince of the Apostles and a spokesman of the Apostolic band. I do not myself believe that this concept of unity is so remote from the Orthodox one as some of my Orthodox brethren appear to hope. I say 'hope' advisedly, for the fear of which I spoke earlier has encouraged many to underline the undoubted differences which do exist between Orthodox and Catholics, in an effort to keep at bay what seems to them the absorption into the Roman Communion. Yet the *koinonia [communion]* of the Apostles, which I have used to characterize the Orthodox pattern of unity, is certainly present in the Roman Communion. The absence of the Eastern Churches since the Great Schism, and the claim to supremacy by the successors of St. Peter, may obscure to the eyes of the world and to Protestants who have lost both the sense of Apostolic tradition and the desire for it. But it is only on this foundation that the Papal claims can be maintained.

---

2 Helle Georgiadis, "Orthodoxy, Rome and Oecumenism" (*Eastern Churches Quarterly*, 1956–57), 349.

The Roman pattern of unity is also, however, the pattern of the one fold and one shepherd. It was to St. Peter that Our Lord committed the care of His sheep. The sacred charge 'Feed my lambs', 'Feed My sheep' was given to Simon Peter, son of Jonas, repeated indeed three times, after St. Peter had been called to affirm his love of the Lord. I believe that those of us who are outside the Roman Communion will not begin to have a true view of the problem of unity as it confronts the Church of Rome, until we have meditated deeply on this fact and its implication. For the Roman Church has always sought her lost sheep, those sheep which the Lord committed to St. Peter and which have strayed from the one fold through ignorance, stupidity or willfulness. Thus it is absurd, and indeed unjust to blame the Catholic Church for seeking to make converts or to 'proselyte' other Christians.[3]

It was the view of an "infallible magisterium" traditional among the Greek Orthodox which inevitably led her to acceptance of the Papacy as acknowledged in pre-Schism Eastern ecclesiology. To her mind, it was impossible that major historical divisions from the Church known as *schisms* could dissolve the Oneness of the Church's visible Unity and Catholicity. The Church's Unity and Catholicity were by their nature *both internally and externally* indivisible. "*A divided Church cannot be a Catholic Church*", she took note to observe in another article before becoming Catholic.[4] The tradition preserved in the Orthodox Churches testified to Christ's Church possessing an infallible magisterium (i.e., the Episcopate) specifically designed by Christ to safeguard its Unity and Catholicity: "*Both Orthodoxy and Rome hold with unswerving conviction that the Church's magisterium [its Episcopate] is absolute in character and therefore unique and invested with the infallible authority of God in Christ.*"[5] However, she became aware that some Russian Orthodox theologians and philosophers had developed the-

---

3 Helle Georgiadis, *Eastern Churches Quarterly*, Autumn 1950.
4 Helle Georgiadis, "Orthodoxy, Rome and Oecumenism," 356.
5 Ibid., 349.

ories which eliminated infallibility from the hierarchical episcopate. If the Church were not to become an invisible reality, she came to realize that an infallible magisterium held to be absolutely necessary to the Church was not possible unless there was an enduring and permanent visible organ of infallibility possessing the supreme authority to teach and rule all the Church's faithful including the bishops. The Papacy alone in the person of Peter and his successors, the Bishops of Rome, had an historical claim to be that supreme authority which Christ established to safeguard the visible unity of his Church. Moreover, the acts of the first seven Ecumenical Councils indicated that the Episcopate of the one Church gathered in an Ecumenical Council could be infallible only in communion with its visible head and center of unity. In short, Miss Georgiadis became aware that the Church as a visible society could not be conceived as possessing a visible unity without a *visible center of unity* manifested in the headship of Peter and his successors. This pattern of Peter's headship was revealed in Scripture itself. A purely spiritual or mystical union of Bishops *at odds with the authority of the Church's Chief Bishop serving as the Rock of the Episcopate* could not constitute that Visible Unity with which Christ endowed His Church. The Orthodox themselves stressed the truth taught by the Fathers of the Church that the supreme model and principle of the Church's visible Unity was the undivided Unity of the Trinity. But only a visible Church graced by the Pope's headship and supreme authority could manifest itself as the visible sign of the Undivided Unity of the Trinity. In 1960 she observed,

> Undoubtedly the Orthodox Churches have suffered through the schism with Rome and the development of the spiritual life has been hampered. Moreover, they have lost not only the reality but the symbol of unity as expressed through the Pope as Christ's Vicar. And though the reality is more important, the loss of symbol obscures the vision which prompts men to seek the reality.[6]

---

6 Helle Georgiadis, Unity and the Eastern Churches, (*The Life of the Spirit*, 1960), 341–342.

A world-wide Church lacking a visible head and center of unity could not possibly be identified as the One visible Body of Christ commissioned to "make disciples of all nations" (Matt. 28:19). Writing in the English Catholic periodical, *The Tablet*, Miss Georgiadis noted the effect of schism in compromising the very principle of Church infallibility occurring with the confusion and contradictions evident among certain theologians (especially Russians):

> Most of the present-day Orthodox have little understanding of Papal infallibility, but they accept the principle of the Church's infallibility. . . . [Yet] the fact is that the Orthodox have no defined or explicit ecclesiology. Some of the younger Russian emigre theologians, aware of the difficulty, have attempted to formulate one on the basis of the existing practice of autonomy among the Orthodox Churches.[7] But such attempts are personal and tentative. Patriarch Athenagoras has worked hard to bring the Orthodox Churches together to study this and other problems. The traditional Orthodox appeal to the first seven Ecumenical Councils to find the norms of Orthodox faith and practice no longer meets the pressing needs of twentieth-century Christendom. In spite of the two pan-Orthodox gatherings at Rhodes in the last three years there are no signs yet of anything approaching an Orthodox General Council which alone could elucidate an accepted ecclesiology for the Orthodox.
>
> Recently, the Orthodox Bishops in Greece have spoken bitterly about the Church of Rome, and it is worth recalling that this is not the only Greek view. Mr. Bail Moustakis, then secretary of the Association of Orthodox Christian Lay Theologians, wrote in an article[8] in *Anaplassis*: 'The Primacy of the Bishop of Rome is an indisputable histori-

---

7 See, for example, J. Meyendorff, A. Schmemann, et. al., *The Primacy of Peter* (Faith Press, 1963).
8 Bail Moustakis, article in *Anaplassis* (reprinted in *Vers l'Unite chretienne*, April, 1960).

cal fact. No scientific or ecclesiastical value can be attached to the attempts of the anti-Papal critics to cast doubt upon this evident truth ... hence Primacy as such should not be looked upon as an obstacle to reunion.' He also defended Papal infallibility and saw no obstacle in the Filioque, purgatory, or the dogmas of the Immaculate Conception and Assumption, that should stand in the way of reunion. This is a personal view not shared by many Orthodox, but his article aroused great interest in Greece and a surprising amount of sympathy.[9]

The various post-Vatican II theological dialogues between Catholics and Orthodox from Rhodes (1960) to Ravenna (2007) have engendered even more sympathy among the various Orthodox jurisdictions for Unity with the Catholic Church (not to overlook the strident protests of Athonite monks and some prelates resulting in strong rebukes from the Ecumenical Patriarch of Constantinople Bartholomew I). The words of Helle Georgiadis written in 1979 provided serious thought for both traditionalists and modernists whom she saw distorting both the letter and spirit of Vatican II. Her comments have special application to those ultra-traditionalist Orthodox who misunderstand Holy Tradition in seeking to reduce the Primacy of the Roman Pontiff to a mere "Primacy of honor" while ignoring the reality of doctrinal progress in the life of the hierarchical Church:

> In every generation the attention of the faithful is directed by the Holy Spirit to facets of Truth contained in Holy Tradition which have been forgotten, or have been passed over unnoticed. Holy Tradition was not given to the Church to be locked-away in an air-conditioned storeroom, as some traditionalists of strict observance often seem to imply; nor to be relegated to the glass cases of a museum of antiquities, which modernists assume to be its proper resting place.

---

9 Helle Georgiadis (*The Tablet*, April 4, 1964), 374.

> Holy tradition is not a textbook of dogma and canon law: it is the treasure-house of the Revelation of Christ entrusted to the Church. For this reason the Church must guard the integrity of Tradition, keep it unblemished by false accretions, and approach it with humility and reverence and the confidence of faith, knowing that the Revelation of God in Christ is already complete, though the mortal eyes of the faithful have yet to see its perfection.[10]

Helle Elpiniki Georgiadis was an outstanding worker for Christian Unity who realized that every baptized person has the obligation to cooperate in the recomposition of unity among all those who believe in Christ, that is, the Unity of the Church which is professed in the Creed. Possessing a remarkable grasp of the ethos of Protestantism and Greco-Russian Orthodoxy, she manifested a love of the Catholic Church always inspired by the words of her beloved Liturgy of St. John Chrysostom that was often celebrated by a Belorussian priest at Marian House in London and which she often attended: *"Let us love one another, that with one mind we may confess: The Father, Son and Holy Spirit, Trinity, One in essence and undivided."*

The witness of Helle Georgiadis to the visible Unity of the Church may be said to have been an important response to the stirring words of the saintly Byzantine Greek Catholic Bishop Georges Calavassy (1881–1957) who became noted for his works of charity that won the respect of many Orthodox. In the early 1920's he helped thousands of refugees in a general exchange of populations that took place between Greece and Turkey, and helped organize despite opposition from the Greek Orthodox hierarchy the Byzantine Greek Catholic Church in Greece with an Exarchate established in Athens. He was of a long line of Greek *"Enotiki"* (unionists) before and after the famous Council of Florence (1439). In one of his memorable addresses, he cried out:

---

10 Helle Georgiadis, Sacramental and Charismatic Ministries: Papal Auithority and Christian Unity, (*The Clergy Review*, May 1979), 161.

In the name of God, in the name of the Church of Christ, in the name of the whole of Christendom, in the name of our beloved country and of our nation, I beg you Christians and Greeks, to shake off the lethargy to which indifference to the problem of union has made you captive. See clearly the disastrous consequences of our disunion, measure the advantages of union, stir up in yourselves a desire for unity and put this into action according to the possibilities open to you. A united Christianity! What an invincible force! What happiness lies in store for all mankind when East and West are once again united! What a wonderful victory, too, for the Greek Church and for Hellenism! And above all what a triumph for the Divine Founder of the Church when the desire of His Sacred Heart is fulfilled 'that all may be one.'[11]

---

11 Bishop Georges Calavassy, Address, found in *Unitas* vol. 6 (Society of the Atonement, 1954).

Chapter X
Helene Iswolsky (1896–1975)

Noted author, historian, journalist and translator, Helene Iswolsky, was born Elena Alexandrovna Iswolsky, on July 24, 1896, in Germany, as the daughter of Russian Statesman and Foreign Minister Alexander Iswolsky and Countess Marguerite Toll, descendant of a general who fought Napoleon's invasion of Russia.[1] Her father held various diplomatic posts at the Holy See, Belgrade, Munich, Tokyo, and Copenhagen, and when World War I broke out was Czar Nicholas II's Ambassador to Paris. Living in France, Helene made her academic studies in law and economics which resulted in a life-long interest in political, social, and religious questions. She herself was

---

1 Sources: *Helene Iswolsky, Light Before Dusk: A Russian Catholic in France 1923–1941* (New York: Longmans, Green and Co., 1942);

Helene Iswolsky, *No Time To Grieve: An Autobiographical Journey from Russia to Paris to New York,* Foreword by Marguerite Tjader (Philadelphia, PA: The Winchell Company, 1985);

Helene Iswolsky, *Soul of Russia* (London, Sheed & Ward, 1944);

Helene Iswolsky, *Christ in Russia: The History, Tradition and Life of the Russian Church* (Milwaukee: The Bruce Publishing Company, 1960).

brought up Russian Orthodox, though her father had no deep adherence to the established Church, and her mother always remained a Protestant. On his deathbed, her father refused the administration of an Orthodox priest, calling instead upon the services of his wife's Lutheran pastor. When her father died in 1919, surprised by the outbreak of the Bolshevik Revolution, the family was deprived of the lifestyle formerly enjoyed which had allowed Helen time and leisure for travels. Helene was obliged to seek work as a journalist and would continue to live in France until 1941 when the Nazi occupation forced her to leave. During those years as she recounted in her autobiography *No Time to Grieve: An Autobiographical Journey from Russia to Paris to New York*[2], she would make contact with some of the most distinguished cultural figures of the time such as Charles du Bos, Paul Claudel, Gabriel Marcel, Paul Valery, Jacques Riviere, and became an intimate friend of the French philosopher Jacques Maritain, and the Russian philosopher Nicholas Berdaiev. She wrote of these friends and contacts: "They taught me to think with clarity and to write with precision." Helping to confront the spreading propaganda of Nazism and Communism, she wrote two books in French (*Soviet Man Now* and *Soviet Women*) denouncing Soviet suppression of the human dignity of men and women. She translated into French the Russian works of Nicholas Berdiaev, Alexander Blok, Peter Krassnov, the poet Wenceslaus Ivanov, and others; translated into Russian the work of the editor of the personalist review *Esprit*, Emmanuel Mounier; and translated important books by Russian writers Michael Bachtin, Alexander Kerensky, and Fr. Alexander Elchanninov into English. She may be said to have incarnated in her person an entire cultural period evidencing a French Catholic revival, the vicissitudes of Russian emigres to the West, and the first spiritual and intellectual contacts between Orthodox and Catholics. Her earlier book *Light Before Dusk: A Russian Catholic in France, 1923–1941: Recollections* gives a fascinating account of her life in France, her love of both Russia and France, her numerous ecumenical contacts with priests and laity, and her many friendships among Catholics and Orthodox. As her dear friend Mar-

---

2 Iswolsky, *No Time to Grieve*.

guerite Tjaer who accompanied her on her last trip to Russia, noted in the ecumenical review *Diakonia:*

> The themes of her life became her passionate love for Russia and her desire for the unity of all Christians.... Helene's book, *Light Before Dusk*, is a dramatic and utterly engrossing account of that teeming, creative period in Paris, just before the disaster of World War II. In it she tells how, in Paris, she began to study and discuss the ideas of Vladimir Soloviev, philosopher at the turn of the century, who was far ahead of his time. His *Russian Idea* and *Russia and the Universal Church* were already classics and he himself lived his own convictions. *'Union of the Churches was at the center of his life'*, wrote Helen and described how he had made himself an example of unity by asking to be taken into the Catholic Church in Moscow by a priest of the Eastern rite, Fr. Nicholas Tolstoy. This was done in secrecy, for there was no freedom of religion in those days. A Russian was forbidden to renounce Orthodoxy. Later, when Soloviev was dying in the country, it was not safe to summon a Catholic priest for the same reason and an Orthodox Father gave him the last rites. His ideas are acceptable to the Russian Catholic as they are to the Russian Orthodox and form an organic link between them. Soloviev was a friend of Dostoyevsky, Constantine Leontiev and Feodorov, Russian thinkers who deeply influenced modern Russian philosophy.
>
> How often Helene spoke and wrote of Soloviev! She had his picture in her room, an intense, brooding, magnetic face. When she visited Moscow in 1961, she found his grave in the Novo Devichy Monastery and stooped down to put some soil from it in an envelope which she had prepared. She treasured this afterwards, asking that it be emptied on her own grave. This, friends were able to do, when she died last December and was laid to rest in the Catholic Worker plot of the country cemetery at Tivoli, New York. Certainly, Soloviev was one of the greatest

influences guiding her life and the work of *The Third Hour* [*her ecumenical journal that would be published in the USA*].³

In *Light Before Dusk* she noted:

> Though nominally an Orthodox, I had lived long enough in France to be familiar with the Catholic Church; it inspired me with respect and admiration, but it did not definitely attract me. On the other hand, Orthodoxy did not seem to give any answer to the religious problems which had begun to loom before me, as for many young people of the war generation. I had always been a believer, but there was a veil drawn between me and the God I worshipped.⁴

That veil began to be lifted in stepping into the "unknown world" of the cloistered Benedictine Abbey of St. Scholastica in the Toulouse region. This she explained in greater detail in her fuller autobiography *No Time to Grieve*. There she met Mother Eustochie, a Russian who had become a Catholic, and though living in the monastery for twenty-five years, had not forgotten her native tongue. She had been a devout Orthodox, was familiar with Russian monastic life, and occupied with how best to bring about the Reunion of the Churches. Then began *"a correspondence which brought new light into my troubled soul; how was I to reconcile East and West, the Orthodox faith and the Catholic? How to find the peace of mind that eluded me?"*⁵ She was comforted by Mother Eustochie's explanation of the intimate connection of Benedictine religious life with Greek and Russian monasticism, and that Russians must not be denationalized to become Latin Catholics but rather retain their liturgical rite and spiritual customs as Russian Catholics. Already acquainted with the perspective of the Russian philosopher Vladimir Soloviev, she realized that East and West were not to be opposed to each other. *"I had read his remarkable works before meeting with Mother Eustochie, who had also been inspired by*

---

3 *Diakonia*, vol. II, no. 11, [1976].
4 Iswolsky, *Light Before Dusk*, 15.
5 Iswolsky, *No Time to Grieve*, 149.

*him."*⁶ Later, she would study Soloviev's writings in greater depth with the assistance of another Russian Catholic, Alexandra B., concluding with Soloviev that,

> There is one Universal Church whose head is the Sovereign Pontiff, in accordance with the words of the Gospel, 'There shall be one fold and one shepherd' and, 'Thou art Peter, and on this Rock I shall build My Church.' Even those who dispute his actual union to Rome cannot fail to recognize that these lines of the Gospels form the basis of Soloviev's religious thought, for he often expressed it in his writings. . . . This recognition of St. Peter's successors as the supreme judges in matters of religion logically infers the acknowledgment of the dogmas established by Rome, and especially in this case of the dogmas which the Orthodox Church has failed to recognize, such as the Filioque, and the Immaculate Conception. Concerning the latter, it must be remembered that the doctrine of the Immaculate Conception is of Eastern origin and exists in the Orthodox church as 'a free theological opinion.' Therefore, the difficulties of admitting this dogma by the Orthodox are very much exaggerated. The real difficulties exist elsewhere, and Vladimir Soloviev was the first to grasp them.⁷

For Helene Iswolsky, Soloviev would always be *"my master."* It was on September 14, 1923, on the Feast of the Exaltation of the Holy Cross, that she was finally received into the Catholic Church. She laid bare her soul to Dom Romain Benquet who was the saintly spiritual director and confessor of the Benedictine nuns of St. Scholastica:

> I felt [he] knew human nature better than any psychologist I had known. There was something of the Cure d'Ars about him, or of Dostoyevsky's Father Zosima. . . . I had been away from the Sacraments for at least ten years. When asked why I became a Catholic, I answered, 'I wanted to

---

6 Ibid.
7 Iswolsky, *Light Before Dusk*, 54, 57.

get back to the Sacraments.' The Catholic Church helped me to do so at the time of a complete spiritual blackout. It was as simple as that.[8]

She did not minimize the dogmatic reasons that led her fellow Russians to become Catholics, reasons that had led her "master" Soloviev to reject the wild anti-Catholic invectives and exaggerations of Dostoyevsky and Komiakhov and other Slavophile theologians. But Soloviev was not the only Russian philosopher and writer to take issue with extreme Russian nationalists who only perpetrated the grievances of medieval Greeks. There was also the writer Vassililij Vassilievitch Rosanov (1856–1919) who was brought up in a strongly anti-Catholic environment, held some heterodox views but died a Russian Orthodox. His studies led him to find repugnant that "extraordinary feeling of irritation in the East against the West. . . . Byzantium whispered in the ear of Russia that Catholics are not even Christians."[9] Though retaining many anti-Catholic prejudices, he gave this remarkable testimony to the Papacy:

> After the death of the Savior, Peter had already returned to his trade of fisherman, and perchance he knew nothing of Rome, of its political-geographic importance; but now he hastened to go to Rome and die on the Cross as did his Savior. It is on this second Cross, that of Peter, on which was raised the Lateran, a Vatican, the Basilica of St. Peter. In that triple 'Feed My sheep' the whole Papacy is contained like the corollary of a theorem. Yes, the Roman Primacy is the mantle of Elijah. Our [Orthodox] theologians have never succeeded in explaining the meaning of those words of Christ. Like parrots, they obstinately repeat vacuous and

---

8   Iswolsky, *No Time to Grieve*, 155.
9   S. Tyskiewicz, SJ, Reflexions du penseur russe V. Rosanov sur le catholicisme, (*Nouvelle Revue de Theologie* (Dec. 1952), 1062–1074). Even more striking passages on Papal supremacy by
Rosanov are given in Charles Journet, *The Primacy of Peter* (Westminster, MD: The Newman
Press, 1954); 113–115.

at bottom nihilist phrases". 'All the Apostles were equal'; 'Between them there is no difference in authority or dignity' '. . . All Bishops are equal, and the Bishop of Rome is equal to the Bishop of Kalouga.' All such reasoning offends Russian honesty!

Let us go to the text of the Gospel cited above: 'I do not understand,' you say; 'I see, but I do not wish to consent to it.'. . . All Christianity was always pyramidal and hierarchical, ascending towards one chief shepherd, and not several. . . . True, there is a shepherd at Kalouga, at Moscow, at Constantinople; but he has proved successful only in Rome where Peter was led in spirit, where he died, where he conquered the Colosseum, overthrew the Emperors, and founded a Kingdom that is not of this world.[10]

Helene always refused to engage in polemics, recalling the words of a French priest assigned to the *Eglise des Etrangers* in Paris who was aware of Orthodox sensitivities: "Do not seek occasions for dogmatic discussions and debates with your Orthodox friends. These will only lead to new and more dangerous misunderstandings. Develop your own inner spiritual life and make your home a real Christian home. Let each Orthodox who visits you find an atmosphere of peace and good will. There is more convincing truth in what you are, than in what you say."[11] She avoided open confrontation on religion and politics, thereby receiving the trust of her Orthodox friends who were attracted by her warm sympathy, gentle demeanor, wisdom, unbiased judgment, and obvious love of Russia and fellow Russians.

With the Nazi invasion of France, Helene and her mother fled into Spain and then arrived in the United States, being welcomed by Alexandra Tolstoy, the youngest daughter of the great novelist, to live on her farm. There Helene was able to resume her literary career, writing articles on Russian culture and the Russian people's spiritual resistance to Soviet ideology. She also renewed contacts with her former friends in Paris, such as the Maritains, meeting leading Catholic

---

10 Ibid, 113–115.
11 Iswolsky, *Light Before Dusk*, 64.

intellectuals, and forming intimate friendships with two of the most remarkable women in North American Catholicism, Dorothy Day of the Catholic Worker and Baroness Catherine de Hueck Doherty who would found Madonna House in Canada. Both her new friends were read in the great Russian classics and influenced by the writings of Vladimir Soloviev. A common love of Russian literature and Soloviev's writings drew them together. Helene once said to Dorothy Day that Soloviev was "the prophet of ecumenism and indeed of everything good in Russia." Supported by her many friends, Helene would edit nine issues of *The Third Hour*, a pioneer quarterly ecumenical publication to which prominent Catholics, Orthodox, and Protestants contributed and sought to further Christian unity and peace. Regular meetings of the most diverse people interested in *The Third Hour's* spiritual and intellectual encounters were held in her home as well as in churches. As one of her confreres related: "We were perhaps the first here to publish articles on Simone Weil, Edith Stein, Mother Maria Skobtsov, [a Russian Orthodox nun], Teilhard de Chardin, Mounier, and Feodorov. Theologians like Berdyaev, Maritain, and Karl Barth participated in the magazine." Realizing the need for more financial support, Helene became a journalist for the French desk of the Voice of America, an Instructor in Russian Literature at Fordham University (1949–1956) and professor at Seton Hill College where she was awarded an honorary degree in Humanities. Her books *The Soul of Russia* (1944) and *Christ in Russia* (1960) introduced an English-speaking public to Russian history and culture and the rich monastic spirituality of the Russian people whose Orthodoxy was rooted in the Catholic tradition held in common by the Western and Eastern Fathers of the undivided Church. When she retired from teaching, she continued her ecumenical labors with her *The Third Hour* journal, the writing of articles, giving lectures, making contacts with ecumenists here and abroad, and living at Dorothy Day's Catholic Worker farm at Tivoli, New York. She spent her last days at the home she called the Ben-Serg Center in honor of her beloved St. Benedict and St. Sergius. There in Cold Spring, NY., surrounded by the books of her Library, she hoped it would serve also as a center for

Russian studies and Third Hour meetings. Near a small Benedictine monastery, she was enabled to drink again of the Benedictine spirit which gave peace to her soul. Brother Victor, one of the Benedictine monks, would write:

> It is hard to describe what her own little Center meant to Helene and how much happiness it brought her in the last years of her life. There she lived a life of prayer, study, work, and hospitality. We often came there to pray with her, to sing Compline in the icon corner of her bedroom. We realized that she was immersed in an intense life of union with Christ, a life hidden in Him. She often told us that Christ was always with her, her friend and companion., that she walked and talked with Him. This did not prevent her from caring for her other responsibilities. Every day, for three or four hours, she worked on translations, to supplement her small income. She did this, up to the last day in her Center, when she had a fall and was taken to the hospital.

Helene Iswolsky died on December 24, 1975, after six weeks in the hospital. She was buried in a Benedictine habit given by the nuns of Regina Laudis monastery. Her devoted friend, Marguerite Tjader, wrote: "She was indeed 'Sr. Olga,' an oblate of St. Benedict. After her death, many remarked at the extraordinary serenity of her face, like that of a Russian icon."

In 1976 appeared the 10th issue of *The Third Hour*.[12] Reviewer James Kritzeck observed fittingly, "Cut out to be a *grande dame* in a worldly way, she chose instead to become a saint, the way Leon Bloy and the Maritains (and Charles Peguy and Henri Gheon) understood the popular meaning of the term, which was quite the way the Russian church understood it."

Like her "master" Vladimir Soloviev, Helene Iswolsky believed that the task of reunion was particularly obtainable between Orthodox and Catholics. With works of charity and ecumenical sensitivity,

---

12 Thomas E. Bird et al., eds., *The Third Hour: Helen Iswolsky Memorial Volume* (New York: 1976), 142.

she pursued Soloviev's "The Russian Idea," i.e., the mission of the Russian people tried and purified by the sufferings of the 20th century to participate in the Petro-centric Unity of the Universal Church.

Chapter XI
Count George Bennigsen (1879–1962)
(Georgij Pavlovich Bennigsen)

Count George Bennigsen was born in Russia in 1879 and became a Catholic in 1925.[1] Living in England, he participated in various conferences in England to acquaint Catholics with the plight of persecuted Christians under Bolshevik rule and to foster prayer and study for the eventual reunion with Rome of a Russian Orthodoxy enslaved under Communism. In 1926 and 1930 he wrote some remarkable articles in the Dominican periodical *New Blackfriars* giving a history of the Friars-Preachers in Russia from the 13th century (with St. Hyacinth)

---

1   Sources: Religion in Russia: Cambridge Russian Summer School Lectures, 1939 (Ed. with Intro. by Count George Bennigsen). (London: Burns, Oates & Washbourne Ltd., 1940);

Count George Bennigsen, The Friars-Preachers in Russia (*New Blackfriars*, July 26, 422–434; August 26, 504–514; September 1926, 568–576);

J.N. Danzas, *The Russian Church* (New York: Sheed & Ward, 1936).

Martha Edith Almedigen, BA, *The Catholic Church in Russia Today* (New York: P.J. Kennedy And Sons, 1923).

to the Russian Revolution. Various papers dealing with the history of Russia and the religious scene under Communist oppression as well as the future prospects for a future Catholic apostolate read at the Cambridge Summer School of Russian Studies in 1939 were edited by Count Bennigsen and published as *Religion in Russia*.[2] He was active as a member of the executive committee of the Society of St. John Chrysostom. His wife Countess Olga Bennigsen (born 1879) translated the important work *The Russian Church* by Julia Danzas,[3] as well as some essays by the Russian philosopher Nikolai Berdiaev that were published in the volume *The Bourgeois Mind and other Essays*.[4] In the introduction to his book *Religion in Russia*, Count Bennigsen observed how godless and totalitarian Communism had perverted the Orthodox/Slavophile idea of "The Third Rome":

> National pride [of the Russian people], as expressed in the idea of the Third Rome and the messianic dream of the Slavophiles and their present-day followers who still insist upon the universal mission of the Russian Church 'so providentially helped by the dispersion of millions of Russians abroad', has been realized in a most unexpected way in the perverted messianic reality of the Third International. Lenin's idea of a world revolution wherein Russia is to play the leading part is but the logical outcome of the Third Rome theory, whilst Communism has achieved the final triumph of State over Church by first freeing the secular power of all moral obligations towards God and His Church, and then finally decreeing the abolition of all religion and the State's absolute supremacy.

With the unexpected collapse of the atheistic Soviet Empire in 1989–1991 and new freedom granted the Russian Orthodox Church as well as the efforts undertaken by the Second Vatican Council to renew

---

2 *Religion in Russia*, ed. by Count Bennigsen (London: Burns Oates & Washbourne Ltd., 1940).
3 Julia Danzas, *The Russian Church* (Sheed & Ward, 1936).
4 *The Bourgeois Mind and other Essays*, edited by Donald Attwater (Sheed & Ward, 1934).

the bonds of ancient friendship between the See of Rome and the Churches of the East (both Oriental Orthodox and Eastern Orthodox), there has in our time resulted genuine theological progress via ecumenical dialogues seeking to overcome dogmatic differences. In the Joint International Catholic-Orthodox Commission such as that which took place in Ravenna, Italy, in 2007) Eastern Orthodox representatives are seen to no longer dispute the historical fact of a Universal Primacy being exercised by the Roman Pontiff from the beginnings of the Church. Nevertheless, despite a welcome openness to the to the idea of a universal Petrine Primacy in the Church, there remains resistance to the Catholic doctrine that the Primacy of the holy Roman Church is not of human or ecclesiastical arrangement but rather of divine institution. Moreover, in Catholic doctrine, it cannot be a Primacy that has been lost because of heresy over the Procession of the Holy Spirit as claimed by such prominent 14th and 15th century Byzantine Greek theologians as Nilus Cabasilas and Symeon of Thessalonica. In the following paper read at the Reunion Society, Oxford, in 1932 and published in *The Catholic World* in 1934, Count Bennigsen gives voice to the immemorial doctrine of the Catholic Church concerning the Roman Primacy in the Church. That doctrine, as all know, has been firmly set forth in the great Ecumenical Councils of Florence, Vatican I, and Vatican II. The views he presented in this article concerning Catholic-Orthodox relations remain as true today with the exception of Vatican II's allowing the access of Orthodox in spiritual need to the Sacraments of Penance, Eucharist, and Anointing of the Sick. Particularly interesting is Count Bennigsen's having observed astutely in his *Catholic World* article (that follows in full) that there had developed sharp divisions between Russian and Greek theologians and between Russian theologians themselves over the hierarchical nature of the Church and its infallibility. The 1970 Ravenna international dialogue which saw the Russian delegates walk out in a dispute over the patriarchate of Constantinople's claim to be the leader of the Orthodox world, has revealed the continuance of the serious internal divisions between traditionalist and modernist theologians that prevent agreement resulting in a coherent Orthodox ecclesiology.

"The Orthodox Church and Reunion"
(From *The Catholic World*, 1934)

The disunion which is witnessed in our days [1932] among Christians is a matter of deep concern to all sincere believers, and the inability of men to return to the unity which was the subject of Our Lord's last prayer is one of the strongest weapons in the hands of the enemies of Christianity. This abnormal position of the Christian world is acutely felt not only by the leaders but also by the rank and file of all Christian denominations and attempts to restore the lost unity are made throughout the world. In order to grasp them, and to appreciate their full significance it is, however, necessary to understand clearly the principles which underlie these attempts when we speak of the 'Reunion of Churches' or of the 'Reunion of Christianity' with members of another denomination we must first of all be clear as to whether our conception of Christianity and of the Church is identical with theirs. Otherwise, our discussions will be futile, and only lead to an exchange of polite compliments or to useless polemics. Therefore, it seems necessary at first to see what Catholics and Orthodox understand by the word 'Church.'

They both believe alike that the Church is a divinely instituted society including the living and the dead, and also spiritual beings—the angels. The Church, therefore, is both visible and invisible. The visible Church or the Church on earth, has a certain organization which again Orthodox and Catholics alike hold is divinely instituted. They believe that the Church is founded on a hierarchical principle which means that certain of her members are endowed with certain spiritual rights and powers given them by virtue of a special grace (the Orthodox call it 'charisma') conferred through an unbroken succession of Bishops descending from the Apostles to whom this power was given by Our Lord Himself. They believe that the visible Church has a visible organization consisting of the shepherds—the bishops with their assistants—the priests and deacons, and the flock—the laity. The hierarchy established by Christ is to teach men to observe all things whatsoever He has commanded (Matt. 28: 19–20), and to dispense the Holy Sacraments (Matt. 28: 19); Luke 10: 16) and to believe them (Mark 16: 16).

Both Catholics and Orthodox believe that the Church is a Kingdom with Christ as its King (Matt. 13), as a house built on a rock (Matt. 6: 24–27), a fold into which all sheep are to be brought (John 10: 14–16). The Church for Catholics and Orthodox alike is more than an organization or a mere society—it is a living organism, the Body of Christ. Its Head and the only Head of the whole Body, visible and invisible, is Our Lord Himself (Eph. 5: 23). It is activated and receives grace, or its actual life, from the Holy Spirit who descended on the Apostles on the day of Pentecost.

We can see up to now there is no difference in the doctrine of Catholics and Orthodox upon the Church. However, the difference appears when we further examine the organization of the *visible* Church. Catholics believe that Our Lord has given special powers to one of His Apostles—Peter, and that these powers, like the powers of all other Apostles, are transmitted to St. Peter's successors. They believe that, having chosen one amongst the twelve, Christ entrusted to him His lambs and His sheep. (John 21: 15–17) which signifies not only the power of feeding them but also of teaching, for 'the sheep hear his (the shepherd's) voice,' and the sheep follow him 'because they know his voice' (John 10: 3–4). He was given the power of confirming his brethren (Luke 21: 32); on him as upon the rock Christ built His Church against which the Gates of Hell shall not prevail, for Christ is with His Church 'all days even to the consummation of the world' (Matt. 16:

18; 28: 20); to him Christ gave the keys of the Kingdom of Heaven—the great symbol of authority.

This organization of the Church, being a question 'de fide' for Catholics, conditions their whole attitude in the matter of Reunion. The visible Church is one and undivided. She consists of members professing the same faith expressed in the doctrine formulated by the Church's teaching body, the hierarchy headed by the Successor of St. Peter. The essential thing is unity of faith. To guarantee this unity of faith Our Lord instituted an infallible center of unity. People outside the Church often misunderstood the meaning of the powers of St. Peter which is nothing else than a special *charisma* preventing him and his successors from erring in matters of faith—a gratuitous grace, without which, as we shall see further, no guarantee of any infallibility in the Church can exist at all.

The number of faithful within the Church may be large or small: at the beginning of Christianity, it consisted of a handful of men, and yet this handful was the Church Universal. No schism or heresy can break the unity of the Church; they merely separate from her visible unity individuals and whole bodies, often headed by the highest dignitaries of the Church. The unity of the Church is not broken thereby, and were the successor of Peter to remain alone with a few faithful to confess the entire Catholic faith, this would be the one, undivided Catholic Apostolic Church.

Outside the Church there is no salvation—this is a principle which often shocks non-Catholics, yet it is one which is shared by the Orthodox. Father Sergius Bulgakov of the Paris Theological Academy declares it to be a self-evident truth deriving from the very essence of the Church.[5] And yet this does not signify that everybody outside the visible unity of the Church will be damned. On

---

5 *Put*. No. IV., 3.

the contrary, the Church has repeatedly declared that those outside this unity cannot be lost except by their own deliberate fault. Therefore, both schism and heresy become a cause of damnation only if the person fully realizes the truth of Catholic teaching but willfully persists in remaining separated from the Church.

The attitude of the Catholic Church towards religious bodies outside its fold varies. Believing herself to be the only true Church, and the whole Church, all others are considered either in schism, if they have not corrupted the doctrine they held at the time of separation, or in heresy if they have. Those that have preserved intact the Sacraments of the Church and their Orders real and valid, though not lawful, may return to the unity of the Church as bodies, or as parts of the Church. To use a metaphor, they are branches of the Vine. The sap still running in them from the Vine to which they belonged once, prevents them from dying; they may be grafted on again to the stem, and be united to it. This is the position of the many Uniate Churches which belong to the unity of the Catholic Church, are one with her in faith, though retaining their local and national characteristics, customs, discipline and way of worship.[6]

It is obvious from what has been said that the condition for the return of the separated bodies to the Catholic Church is a complete submission in all matters of faith. The Church being the guardian of truth cannot but be strict upon questions of *truth*. A Catholic cannot conceive that within the Church, important matters of faith may at

---

6 Note concerning "Uniatism": This is a pejorative term used by Eastern Orthodox who have continually accused the Catholic Church of aggressive proselytism ("stealing Orthodox sheep") to form the Eastern Catholic Churches. The charge of an "unacceptable Uniatism," that is, the establishment of Eastern rite Churches subject to the universal jurisdiction of the Pope within Greece, Russia and other Orthodox countries remains a serious grievance on the part of the Orthodox and hampers objective dialogue and theological discussions between Catholics and Orthodox.

the same time be affirmed and denied—and possessing a divinely instituted center of infallible teaching, he looks to this center every time that the necessity arises for a definite pronouncement.

When we turn to the Orthodox Church, we see also a similar claim of the Orthodox to represent the whole Church possessing the entire unaltered Christian truth. "The Church is indivisible though multiform in her manifestations," says Father Bulgakov.[7] He also notes that "The Church is one, unity is the quality of the Church."[8] "We, Orthodox, believe that the Orthodox Church has preserved intact the fullness of truth of Christ, and cannot, without ceasing to be Orthodox, surrender this faith," says Father Isvolsky.[9] Historically, the only really important difference with the Catholic Church consisted in their rejection of the divinely instituted Primacy and Infallibility of the successors of Peter. For the Orthodox the center of authority and infallible teaching resided theoretically in the Ecumenical Councils. However, upon a deeper study of the question, it becomes much more difficult to answer the query as to what constitutes the unity of the Orthodox Church. The existence of different national Churches must not trouble us too much. One may understand local Churches with various, sometimes very extended rights of self-governance within the one Universal Church provided they are bound together by some uniting principle. No one would deny the existence of this principle in the Catholic Church, but in order to find it in the Orthodox Church we shall quote the words of an Orthodox canonist Professor Tsankov of the University of Sofia who bases his conclusions on the works of the most important Russian and Greek theologians.

'Unity' according to Dr. Tsankov, consists of:

---

7   *Put*, No. 1 1, 68.
8   Ibid.
9   Father Isvolsky, "On Reunion," 4.

> First of all ... in the fact that all belong together inwardly and spiritually to one faith, to the same principles of order and to the same cult. ... To this must be added the consciousness of a common historical past, and then the same religious-ecclesiastical mentality of all Orthodox eastern peoples, as well as the same direction for their religious and Christian tendencies.' Yet, a few sentences further, the same writer adds that as far as the 'inward sense of unity in the Orthodox Churches' is concerned, 'it may seem that this invisible spiritual bond has not always been strong enough nor always permanently effective', and speaking of the outward unity the same writer agrees that 'from a formal and juridical standpoint this question of unity of the Orthodox Churches offers considerable difficulty', and concludes that the 'problem of the constitutional and legal unity of the Orthodox Churches of the present day remains an open one.[10]

It must not be assumed that this vagueness in answering a most important question is a permanent attribute of the Orthodox Church. On the contrary, up to the middle of the nineteenth century Orthodox theologians generally taught that their Church possessed a visible center of authority, infallibility, and therefore of unity in the General or Ecumenical Councils. As is known, there was not a single Ecumenical Council held in the Orthodox Church after their separation from Rome nearly 900 years ago. Some Orthodox theologians have even denied the possibility of a new Ecumenical Council without the participation of the Western Church. But whether possible or not, these Councils were regarded as the supreme power in the Church. The common faith uniting all the members of the Church

---

10 Stepan Tsankov, *The Orthodox Eastern Church*, 96–99.

is that which was taught by the Bishops of the Church assembled in an Ecumenical Council or agreeing upon a question whilst remaining in their dioceses.[11]

Thus, it was clear to all that unity consisted in a recognized center of infallible teaching, and in a definite doctrine, the acceptance of which was necessary for admission to the Communion of the Orthodox Church. In this respect the practice of the Orthodox was precisely the same as that of the Catholic Church. We may draw a parallel in the cases of Vladimir Soloviev and William Palmer of Magdalen College. The former, having arrived at the conclusion of the identity of faith of the Catholic and of the Orthodox Church, considered that by a recognition of the Papal supremacy he automatically became a Catholic without abandoning the Orthodox Church. Soloviev was a theologian and philosopher of great merit, and yet he had to realize that his scheme of intercommunion, if it was really one, had no solid foundation, and finally submitted unconditionally, becoming a Catholic in 1896.[12] William Palmer, believing the faith of the Church of England to be identical with that of the Orthodox Church, travelled to Russia in order to be admitted to Holy Communion in the Orthodox Church without becoming an Orthodox. His request was rejected by the Holy Synod which stipulated that complete recognition of the whole Orthodox doctrine and rejection of all former errors were the necessary conditions for his admittance to the communion of the Orthodox Church. In the same spirit the problem of reunion would have been decided by the Orthodox Church exactly as it is decided now by the Catholic Church—the acceptance by the uniting bodies of the entire doctrine of the Orthodox Church, and recognition of the infallible authority of the Ecumenical Councils.

A change in the whole conception of Orthodoxy was introduced in the middle of the 19th century by the lay theologian Alexis Khomiakov. Anxious to establish an Orthodox theological thought independent of Roman and of Protestant influences, he denied the

---

11 Archbishop Macarius of Kharkov, *Introduction to Orthodox Theology* (*The Catholic World*, 1934), 394, 398, 405, 407, 408.
12 M. d'Herbigny, *Vladimir Soloviev: Un Newman Russe*, 314.

existence of a teaching Church. "*In the true Church,*" he wrote in 1853, "*there is no teaching Church. . . . The separation of the Church into a teaching Church and a Church of pupils (as we should call the lower section), recognized by Romanism as an essential principle . . . has penetrated into Orthodoxy.*"[13] Khomiakov's followers in a way adhered to these views, though less definitely. Father Bulgakov thinks that 'the instructed person is not entirely removed from a participation in the teaching of dogma, as it takes place in Catholicism.'[14] A dangerous development of the teaching consists in the affirmation that the Church does not possess any external organ of infallible teaching. The Ecumenical Councils as such, assure both Khomiakov and Father Bulgakov, whose opinions daily gain ground in the Orthodox Church, are not in themselves such organs, and their decisions become infallible only on their acceptance by the whole body of the Church—Bishops, clergy, and laity alike.[15]

Both writers based their affirmation on a declaration made in 1849 by the Eastern Patriarchs in reply to the Encyclical Letter to Eastern Christians of Pope Pius IX of January 6, 1848. "*We have no secular power,*" wrote the patriarchs, "*but are united in a bond of charity and zeal to our common mother (the Church) in the unity of faith. . . .*" and further: "*With us neither Patriarchs nor Councils could ever introduce anything new, because the guardian of piety is the very body of the Church, i.e., the people itself which always wishes to preserve the faith intact. . . .*"[16]

If even the principles laid down in the declaration were unanimously accepted by the Orthodox Church, which does not seem to be the case, the idea of the necessity of a consensus of the people for the validity of the decisions of the General Councils, shared by the early Gallicans and by the founders of the Old Catholic Schism, if accepted by the Orthodox Church, would mean the end of any

---

13   A.S. Khomiakov, *A Few Words of an Orthodox Christian concerning Western Communions* (Prague: 1867), 55
14   *Put*, No. II, 53.
15   Khomiakov, *Works*, Vol. II (Prague: 1967), 121; Father Bulgakov's articles in *Put*, No. l II, 49–56.
16   Arts. 16 and 17 of the Declaration made in 1849 by the Eastern Patriarchs in reply to the Encyclical Letter to Eastern Christians of Pope Pius IX of January 6, 1848

attempt to develop further doctrine. Already now doctrines which for centuries were accepted by general consent of the whole Orthodox Church as matters of faith are being rejected as matters of private opinions. As no means for testing a "general consensus" of the people can be canonically devised, it is evident that "public opinion" is not a way to decide upon matters of faith, and the change arising in such opinion will make any stability of doctrine impossible.

Whether this new teaching upon Ecumenical Councils will ever be accepted by the whole Orthodox Church is difficult to say, but Professor Tsankov, whom we have already mentioned, thinks that "there can be no doubt that even the bishops sooner or later will bear witness and gave definite expression to what the whole Orthodox Church feels and proves."[17]

All that has been said above leads to the conclusion that Unity in the Orthodox Church is not to be looked for in the Ecumenical Councils. Obviously, we have to look for it in the common faith and in the common faith of the Church. An Orthodox, questioned on this subject, would probably answer that no visible center of unity is required, as unity is preserved by a mystical union of all Orthodox, and manifested in the adherence to a common faith and brotherly love for each other. Naturally when we speak of the common faith, we cannot judge of the internal virtue of faith of the individuals but examine the outward profession of a certain body. Here, again, when examining the doctrine of the Orthodox Church, we are confronted with certain difficulties. What constitutes the *doctrine* of the Orthodox Church? Professor Tsankov declares that *"the dogma of the Church is really of small volume,"* and explains that it consists chiefly in the doctrines of the Ecumenical Councils concerning the Holy Trinity and the Incarnation. He accepts the definition of Professor Bolotov that *"dogma is truth as determined by an Ecumenical Council,"*[18] and seems to relegate all other teachings to the class of 'theologoumena', only probable truths which are not binding the faithful.

Were this teaching to be adopted by the whole Orthodox Church, and certain declarations of so prominent an authority as

---

17 Tsankov, *The Orthodox Eastern Church*, 195
18 Op. cit., 38–40.

Msgr. Meletios, Patriarch of Alexandria, confirm the possibility of its acceptance, the entire Sacramental system and the validity of the Holy Orders might be endangered. Indeed, none of the first seven Ecumenical Councils had defined anything about the Holy Eucharist or the other Sacraments. That this fear is not without foundation can be seen from the development of the teaching on the Holy Eucharist. Professor Tsankov assures his readers that the most various answers are given to such questions as *"What is offered in the Eucharist—the gifts of Christians (the elements) or Christ Himself? Who sacrifices, Christ . . . or the priest, or the Church or . . . the body of the faithful?"* and declares that the doctrine of Transubstantiation *"has never been a dogma of the Orthodox Church."*[19] One cannot be but surprised at these words. Indeed, if there is no authoritative definition as to "What is offered in the Eucharist" or "Who offers the Sacrifice?", these questions are answered by the Liturgy itself. Not a single Liturgy expresses with such unambiguous clearness the central idea that it is Christ Himself Who offers the Holy Sacrifice, and offers Himself as the bloodless Victim, as the Liturgy of St. John Chrysostom.

The doctrine of Transubstantiation was not discussed by any of the first seven Councils; it was defined by the local Council of Jerusalem in 1672 and accepted by the entire Orthodox Church with the exception of its Russian Branch. The Greek text speaks of *metousiosis* which is the equivalent of the Latin *Transubstantio*, and of *symbebeiota* the equivalent of "accidents." When in 1838 the Russian Synod sanctioned for Russia the decisions of the Council of Jerusalem by publishing what was known in Russia as "the Epistle of the Eastern Patriarchs", these two words were omitted. Thus, at a first glance, it would seem indeed that the doctrine of Transubstantiation was unanimously accepted by the whole Orthodox Church. It appears in the same terms in Orthodox Catechisms and manuals of theology and the change made in the text of the "Epistle of the Eastern Patriarchs" is but a verbal one, in nowise affecting the faith. Therefore, the present rejection of the Catholic conception of Transubstantiation

---

19 Op. cit., 117.

by certain Orthodox theologians seems to mark a change in the old Orthodox doctrine.[20]

Other instances might be quoted to show how little modern Orthodox theological thought is restricted by accepted dogma. It seems to be the inevitable result of the fact that development of dogma, as doctrine accepted by the whole Church ceased in the East with its separation from Rome. Father Bulgakov's attempt to emancipate his Church from any Catholic influence which, according to this writer,

> has placed Orthodoxy in a position of indecisive and inconsistent Catholicism, the latter at least having the undisputed merit of consistency, and developing the idea of an external organ of Church infallibility to its ultimate conclusion. The question is precisely to choose between the freedom of Orthodoxy or papism.[21]

Father Bulgakov is certainly right when he deprecates the indecision and inconsistency of his own Church. On the one hand, as we have shown, teachings which have been accepted by the whole body of the faithful are subsequently reversed by the opinion of other generations. On the other, even General Councils, unless their validity and decisions are sanctioned by an outward authority, holding its power by Divine right, can scarcely be acknowledged Ecumenical in themselves. Indeed, we know of Councils (the Ephesus Council of Dioscorus, the Councils of Basle and Constance) convened as Ecumenical and not recognized as such, even declared *"Robber Councils."* Sanction of an Ecumenical Council's decisions by a subsequent Council or by a silent consent of the people, as has been mentioned already, is scarcely possible, and the only workable solution is that which the Catholic Church holds in the letter and spirit of the Holy Gospels. An Ecumenical Council is one which is recognized as such by the Successor of Peter, the Bishop of Rome.

The difficulty of the Orthodox Church realized by Father Bulgakov has led him and other theologians to reject the existence of a

---

20 See *Christian East*, Winter 1930–1931, 163.
21 *Put*, No. II, 49.

recognized center of infallible teaching, and to reduce to a minimum the substance of accepted doctrine. This leads inevitably to a doctrinal comprehensiveness which the Orthodox Church did not know in the past.

We are led to view the prospects of Reunion of the Orthodox Church with other Christian bodies from another angle. Practically this question becomes so much easier to solve as the doctrine becomes less defined and more comprehensive. We have seen above that the Catholic Church, believing herself the only true Church and guardian of the whole truth of Christianity, can consistently demand from other bodies only complete submission and acceptance of her entire doctrine. Owing to the incessantly developing spiritual life of the Church this doctrine, being the same in substance as that of primitive Christianity, has greatly developed in volume. All this developed doctrine has to be accepted by the separated Christians if they wish to be united with the Catholic Church. This is undeniably a difficulty which does not exist with the Orthodox.

A few words should be said on the very actual question of *intercommunion*. The Catholic Church does not admit the possibility of a priest's giving Holy Communion to anybody outside the Church, or of a Catholic's communicating from a minister of another creed. The only exception tolerated is that of a Catholic dying in a foreign land, when he is 'in extremis' he is allowed to receive Holy Communion from an Orthodox priest. The same was the practice of ancient Christianity. Intercommunion presupposed identity of faith, and the Churches which were in communion could be regarded as one Church even when their governing bodies were autonomous. The same principle governs the Orthodox Church of our days, and regular intercommunion can only imply mutual recognition of the respective doctrines as true. Orthodox delegates at Lambeth have explained that Ecumenical intercommunion is not the same as regular intercommunion; yet if whole regions are submitted to such a rule of Oeconomy, it is very difficult to draw the line, and that which today is only an exception will probably become a rule tomorrow.

We see thus that both in the question of intercommunion and in that of reunion a different attitude exists on the part of the Catholic and the Orthodox Churches. The Catholic Church from her whole conception of the Church, her creed, dogma, unity has been brought to a stricter affirmation of the importance of doctrine, including the one on Church authority and infallibility.[22] The Orthodox Church, almost as strict on these questions at the outset, has gradually relaxed this severity and seems to be prepared to be reunited with other Christian bodies on a minimum of dogmatic unity. It is quite evident that as the world stands now prospects of a reunion of Orthodoxy with other Christian bodies are much more promising than the possibilities of a return of these bodies to the Catholic Church.

I cannot refrain from visualizing the effect upon the Catholic Church of a future reunion of the Orthodox with other Christian

---

22 Note on Orthodox participation in Catholic sacraments in view of the "imperfect communion" existing between the Catholic and separated Eastern Churches: Vatican II's Decree on the Catholic Churches of the Eastern Rite noted that, as regards our Eastern brethren, pastoral experience shows that various circumstances affecting individuals can and ought to be taken into account, where the Unity of the Church is not harmed nor are there dangers to be guarded against, but where the need of salvation and the spiritual good of souls are prime considerations. Therefore, the Catholic Church, by reason of circumstances of time, place, and persons, has often followed and still follows a less rigorous course of action, offering to all the means of salvation and a witness, to charity among Christians, through a common sharing in the sacraments, and in other sacred functions and things. (no. 26) ... In view of the principles just noted, Eastern Christians who are separated in good faith from the Catholic Church, if they are rightly disposed and make such request of their own accord, may be given the Sacraments of Penance, the Eucharist and the Anointing of the Sick. Moreover, Catholics may also ask for those same sacraments from non-Catholic ministers in whose church there are valid sacraments, as often as necessity or true spiritual benefit recommends such action, and access to a Catholic priest is physically or morally impossible. (no. 27) (Also see the Pontifical Council for Christian Unity's 1993 Directory for Ecumenism, no. 125–136).

It should be better known that from the 17th into the 20th century Orthodox and Catholics on the Greek islands and in parts of the Middle East received Holy Communion in each other's Churches without such faithful being conscious of dogmatic differences resulting in separated Churches.

Interestingly, except for a brief period after World War II when the Russian Orthodox Church gave permission to its priests to administer the Eucharist to Catholics in spiritual need (later rescinded), the Orthodox Churches do not allow their people to receive Catholic sacraments.

confessions. It has been expressed in certain quarters that when such a reunion takes place, Rome, being faced with another "universal Church" containing the most venerated churches of Christian antiquity, would be compelled to surrender her positions. Yet both Orthodox and Protestants feel that no complete Reunion is possible which would leave outside the Church of Rome. Personally, I think that such a reunion between the Orthodox Church and the Protestant churches, if ever realized, might settle one of the greatest difficulties existing between the Catholic Church and the Orthodox. Father Isvolsky in his little pamphlet mentioned above understood the difficulty. Both the Catholics and the Orthodox believe their respective Churches to be the unique holder of the whole Christian truth.

In other words, each Church believes herself to be the whole Church from which other Churches seceded. Therefore, each expects from the Other a repudiation of her errors, and the return to the truth of the Mother Church. This, according to Father Isvolsky, *"is how the Roman Church acted at each genuine attempt at Reunion, and we must not be astonished that the Orthodox Church should act in the same way."* This means that each Church, if she really believes herself to be the true Church, can demand nothing else but submission. Were the Orthodox as consistent as the Catholics, they would demand complete submission from all other bodies as a condition of reunion, the acknowledgement of their errors, and complete acceptance of the Orthodox teaching. Any other agreement would signify that the Orthodox have surrendered their belief that they consider their Church the only true Church founded by Christ on earth. They would thereby accept the belief that the Church has been broken up into many parts, each holding some fragment of the Divine truth. It is easy to see how this would alter the entire relation between the Catholic Church and the other Christian confessions, even were they united into one body. The Catholic Church alone would be entitled to claim to be the *whole* and *unique* Church of Christ. She alone would be entitled to demand the return of her children to her unity, not the reverse. A "Church" formed of broken fragments would always remain incomplete without the participation of the greatest Church.

In contrast with this incompleteness the unity and unicity of the Catholic Church would become more obvious than ever before.

In his apocalyptic vision of the last days of the world, the great Russian thinker Vladimir Soloviev saw the triumph on earth of the Anti-Christ preaching a gospel of love for humanity's sake. The masses and even the leaders of the Churches apostatize and rally to him. The small groups of faithful Christians—Catholics, Orthodox, and Protestants, headed by the leaders, are compelled to appear before the Seducer, and there, facing death for the profession of their faith in Christ, they consummate the Reunion of Christianity. The venerable John, last Patriarch of the Orthodox recognizes Peter the Apostle in the person of Peter II, the last Pope, and Professor Pauli, head of the Protestants, follows his lead.

Looking at the development of the antichristian movement throughout the world, one is inclined to ask whether Soloviev's vision is not being realized now, and we are faced with a collective Antichrist preaching the hatred of God. Are we then to wait until the last moment to exclaim like the Patriarch of Soloviev's vision: *"Tu es Petrus!"*

CHAPTER XII
James Likoudis[1*] (1928–)
To Be Fully Orthodox is to Be in Communion with Peter's See

Part I

I was born in Lackawanna, NY, in 1928, of a struggling Greek immigrant family from the island of Cephalonia off the west coast of Greece. My father Gerasimos and my mother Katherine owned a

---

1 * James Likoudis, President Emeritus of the lay organization Catholics United for the Faith (CUF) has worked for seven decades to foster the reunion of the Eastern Orthodox Churches with the Catholic Church. He is the author of three additional books and many articles in Catholic publications dealing with ecumenism and the doctrinal obstacles to the restoration of visible unity between the Catholic Church and the separated Eastern Orthodox Churches. His books on this topic are:
The Divine Primacy of the Bishop of Rome: Letters to a Greek Orthodox on the Unity of the Church (Emmaus Road Publishing, 2023); *Eastern Orthodoxy and the See of Peter: A Journey Towards Full Communion*; and *Ending the Byzantine Greek Schism*

small candy and ice cream store at various locations in the old First Ward of the city inhabited by people from many nations who worked mainly at the great Bethlehem Steel Plant (whose smokestacks are now strangely quiet in view of hard times falling upon the steel industry. My parents were Greek Orthodox, and some of my earliest memories were of references to the "Panaghia" (the All-Holy Mother of God), the many signs of the cross made at meals in Byzantine fashion, from right to left, and the majestic and solemn ceremonies of the magnificent Liturgy of St. John Chrysostom which transfixed my soul with a sense of the awesomeness of God and the splendor of His heavenly court. I think it is true from my earliest days that I have never really doubted the existence of God, the divinity of Christ, or the fact that Our Divine Lord had established a visible Church—graces that I attribute to the supernatural virtue of faith received in baptism.

Attending public elementary and high school, I was a bright student, and it was in high school that I began to have a keen interest in religion. Novels such as *Ben-Hur* and *The Robe* excited my imagination, and I wanted to know more about Christ and Christianity. My father did not have a car, and so my family rarely got to church, since our Greek Orthodox church of the Annunciation was miles away in Buffalo. Some of my friends were Catholic, and I felt a sense of jealousy at those who attended the rather mysterious parochial schools I would often pass by in walking home after my own public-school classes. The envy I felt was for their receiving a religious instruction and training denied me. I also developed a certain admiration for the imposing network of Catholic institutions (schools, hospitals, convents, churches) which took care of both the spiritual and material needs of their people. We Orthodox (whether Greeks, Serbs, Bulgarians, Russians, Ukrainians) were far fewer in number than the Catholics of the Latin rite and were badly split into conflicting jurisdictions (with accompanying ethnic rivalries). It frankly never occurred to me to try and frequent regularly another Orthodox church of another ethnic group, closer to home. We were Greek Orthodox, "pure Greeks" (Hellenes), and though we shared a common religion with Orthodox Serbs, Macedonians, and Russians, different languages and customs make it difficult to feel a sense of real solidarity with them. The numerical fewness of Orthodox vis-a-vis Catholics and Protestants as well as the distinct "foreignness" of Greek Orthodoxy in American culture (where religion meant you were either Protestant, Catholic, or Jew) had the effect of at least a partial alienation from my own spiritual and linguistic roots. The "melting pot" of American society even developed a resistance to learning the Greek language better—something I regret to this very day. In addition, the Catholic Church seemed to have accommodated itself to the American cultural milieu far more successfully, though in my high school days I was aware that in a number of ways, Catholics were at odds with the influence of secularism and Protestantism.

In my senior high school year, Catholicism was symbolized for me by the magnificence and Baroque splendor of Our Lady of Victory Basilica in Lackawanna, which was not too far from my school and which I often visited. The Catholic Church was a spiritual force that could not be ignored in my little world; it was both attractive and menacingly formidable since I was aware that Catholics claimed that theirs was the "true Church." I was deeply puzzled by this since my Greek Orthodox Church made the same claim!

It was while a student of history and philosophy at the University of Buffalo (then a private institution) that I began to literally read myself into the Catholic Church. In the Lockwood University Library, the Newman Club had its own special shelf of books dealing with the Catholic faith. I would often find my regular school assignments less interesting than to dip into the fascinating Catholic world of such writers as Cardinals Newman and Manning, Ronald Knox, Father Faber, Belloc and Chesterton, and that marvelous priest-author of the *Masterful Monk* stories, Fr. Owen Dudley. At a time when my secular courses in history and philosophy began to pose all sorts of difficulties regarding historic Christian beliefs, I found in such writers (including St. Thomas Aquinas) a treasure-trove of arguments, and the genius to challenge intellectually their rationalist and skeptical opponents. I delighted in the Masterful Monk's defense of Catholic faith and morals as he combatted the ideology of H.G. Wells, Julian Huxley, and other agnostic or atheist luminaries. I admired the Catholic Church for its intellectualism and its contributions to Western Civilization. I cannot say I understood St. Thomas and Thomism well, but there was no doubt in my mind that the Catholic Church had led its believers to many of the highest achievements of faith and reason. I also was deeply impressed by the remarkable Saints it had produced. I could not reconcile the efflorescence of heroic sanctity in a Church which had succumbed to the heretical depravities and innovations of the devil. Such was the tenor of the encyclical letter issued by the Patriarch Anthimus of Constantinople in 1895 declaring that the Catholic Church "had privily brought into herself through the Papacy various strange and heretical doctrines and innovations, and so she has been torn away and removed far from the true and orthodox Church of Christ."[2] I was in awe at the heights of sanctity reached by St. Thomas Aquinas, St. Bonaventure, St. Francis, St. Dominic, the Jesuit Saints of the Counter-Reformation—St. Ignatius, St. Robert Bellarmine, St. Peter Canisius, St. Andrew Bobola—and such holy souls as St. Bernadette and St. Therese of Lisieux.

My pro-Catholic sympathies were in evidence when the university student newspaper highlighted some violent attacks a-la-Paul Blanshard on the Church regarding the themes of religious liberty, "separation of Church and State," and the Church's alleged opposition to democracy. I was further impressed with the respect (sometimes begrudging) paid the Catholic Church by some of my professors. Whether agnostic, Protestant, or Jewish, these genteel scholars from time to time in their lectures paid due tribute to the impact of the Church on Western thought and civilization (something lacking in too many of their secularist counterparts today). And then there was the slender and stately figure in white of the saintly Pius XII who came to symbolize for me the Church's indomitable struggle to maintain spiritual values in a world that had gone totalitarian and quite mad. It remains my fond hope and prayer that the Angelic Shepherd will one day be declared a Doctor of the Church.

It was in my last university year that I first met my lovely wife Ruth who worked in the university library, and who shared a similar feeling for Catholicism. Her family practiced no religion (her father

---

2 Reply to Pope Leo XIII's "Letter on the Reunion of the Churches".

had been baptized Catholic but had never really practiced the faith, and her mother was vaguely Protestant). She and her brothers and sisters had had no religious upbringing. While in high school, however, she began to attend an Episcopal church whose rector held high Anglican views which were very close to those of Catholics. From the moment I saw her, I loved her.

We often discussed Catholicism. I realized if I were indeed to become a Catholic, and to have a Catholic marriage, I had to resolve once and for all the hesitations I had at submitting to the Catholic Church as the true Church of Jesus Christ. I read everything I could find on the origins of the Schism between the Catholic and Eastern Orthodox Churches, the history and doctrine of the Papacy, and on the Ecumenical Councils of the first eight centuries. One of the books I found, the *Eastern Churches and the Papacy* by the Anglican scholar S. H. Scott, was especially helpful to me, as were the remarkable books on the Primacy of Peter by that great Anglican convert and friend of Cardinal Newman, Thomas William Allies, who spent his life in scholarly defense of the Papacy. Allies confirmed for me once and for all the patristic support for the Primacy of Peter in the early Church.

I also made good use of the wonderful Catholic lending library on the second floor of the Catholic Union building at Main and Virginia in downtown Buffalo. Established many years before by German Catholics to help defend their faith, this lending library was chock-full of Catholic periodicals, newspapers, and a fine assortment of books on the lives of the Saints, spirituality, apologetics, Church history, and every aspect of Catholic faith and morals. I shall never forget the kindness to me of Mr. Cyril Ehenreich who was the library caretaker. He was also in charge of the books sold downstairs in the Catholic Union store. He had a remarkable knowledge of Catholic literature, and I recall the great care he exercised to assure that no doctrinally suspect or morally bad books would be included among his wares. His great love of the Church was evident. He went to his heavenly reward years ago. May his soul rest in the peace of Christ.

It was, therefore, during my last year at university that my views on the Catholic Church, the Papacy, and the Schism between East and West solidified. It was clear—in the words of the Greek lay theologian, Dr. Hamilcar Alivisatos—that "the accumulated indifference, ignorance, suspicions, hate, crimes, and fanaticism of many centuries" since the Crusades had contributed to the growing estrangement between Western and Eastern Christians, a process that culminated in the "cursed schism."

Curiously, such matters as the dogmatic question of the Procession of the Holy Spirit from the Father—*and the Son (Filioque)*—together with the canonical question of the inclusion of the "Filioque" in the Creed—and the use of unleavened bread in the Latin Mass, as well as a host of other liturgical and disciplinary differences—were considered by the medieval Byzantines to be far more important reasons justifying their rupture of communion with the Apostolic See than the repeated claims of Papal supremacy. The great Catholic Czech scholar Fr. Francis Dvornik had shown by his research that the famous Patriarch Photius (often presented as the fervent opponent of Papal supremacy over the entire Church) had actually died in communion with Rome. The latter had never repudiated the teaching of the Popes of his time[3] concerning their succession to the Primacy of Peter whom Our Lord had made the head and center of the Universal Church. By the Orthodox polemicists' own fatal admission that "prior to 1054 the Roman Catholic Church was fully joined to the Orthodox Church," it was evident that the Eastern patriarchates had been in communion with Popes who were unequivocal in declaring their universal jurisdiction over the Church in both East and West. The statement made by dissident writers to our own day that "the Bishop of Rome was *never* at any time accorded any rights or powers over the entire Church" was simply false to the history of the Byzantine Church before 1054 and even to the middle of the 12th century when the first denials of Papal Supremacy began to be made. Pro-Unionist Byzantines continued to defend the Petrine Primacy of the Popes before and after the great Reunion Council of Florence (1439) which at first appeared to have ended three centuries of rupture, discord, estrangement, and formal schism. In his classic work *Russia and the Universal Church* the "Russian

---

3 Popes Nicholas I, Hadrian II, John VIII.

Newman," Vladimir Soloviev, had written powerfully of the Papacy as *"that miraculous ikon of universal Christianity"* demonstrating that the Roman Primacy was of the essence of the Church as a visible institution in the world. Since the Orthodox agreed with Catholics in professing that "the Holy Spirit unfailingly preserves the form of government established by Christ the Lord in the Church,"[4] then the testimony of the early pre-Schism Popes regarding their own role in the Church could not be rejected.

Pope Boniface I (†422) had assuredly summed up the tradition of the earliest centuries when he wrote about the heresies and schisms of his day:

> It is clear that this Roman Church is to all churches throughout the world as the head is to the members, and that whoever separates himself from it becomes an exile from the Christian religion, since he ceases to belong to its fellowship.[5]

The doctrinal teaching of the great Pope St. Leo the Great (†461) on the powers of his See was acknowledged by scholars of every religious persuasion:

> Though priests have a like dignity, yet they have not an equal jurisdiction, since even among the most blessed Apostles, as there was a likeness of honor, so was there a certain distinction of power, and the election of all being equal, preeminence over the rest was given to one, from which type the distinction between the Bishops also has risen, and it was provided by an important arrangement, that all should not claim to themselves power over all, but that in every province there should be one, whose sentence should be considered the first among his brethren; and others again, seated in the greater cities, should undertake a larger care, through whom the direction of the Universal

---

4 Vatican II, *Lumen Gentium*, No. 27.
5 Epistle 14, 1.

Church should converge to the one See of Peter, and nothing anywhere disagree with its head.[6]

Pope St. Gelasius (†496) wrote to the orthodox of his day:

> Yet we do not hesitate to mention that which is known to the Universal Church, namely, that as the See of Blessed Peter the Apostle has the right to loose what has been bound by the judgments of any Bishops, whatsoever, and since it has jurisdiction over every church, so that no one may pass judgment on its verdict, the canons providing that an appeal should be to it from any part of the world, no one is permitted to appeal against its judgment.[7]

Pope St. Agatho (†681) in his famous letter to the 6th Ecumenical Council which was greeted with the acclamation "Peter hath spoken by Agatho," had written the following in full consciousness of the dignity of his See,

> ... Peter's true confession was revealed from heaven by the Father, and for it Peter was pronounced blessed by the Lord of all; and he received also, from the Redeemer of us all, by a threefold commendation, the spiritual sheep of the Church that he might feed them. Resting on his protection, the Apostolic Church [of Rome] has never turned aside from the way of truth to any part of error and her authority has always been faithfully followed and embraced as that of the Prince of the Apostles, by the whole Catholic Church, and by all the venerable Fathers who embraced her doctrine, by which they have shone as most approved lights of the Church of Christ, and [so the Church of Rome] has been venerated and followed by all orthodox Doctors."[8]

---

6 Epistle 14.
7 *Theil*, Epistle 26.
8 *Mansi* XI, 233.

The witness of the great Eastern Saints of the *"undivided Church"* similarly refuted the pretensions that only an empty "Primacy of honor" was envisaged by the famous Petrine texts (Matt. 16: 18–19; Luke 22: 31–32; Jn: 15–17) which singled Peter out to be the Rock-foundation of the Church, the Holder of the Keys of the Kingdom, the Confirmer of his brethren, and the Chief Shepherd of the Church after Christ's Ascension into heaven. In a magnificent passage, St. Maximos the Confessor (†622), one of the greatest of the Byzantine doctors, thus defended the prerogatives of the Roman Church watered with the blood of the Chief Pastor:

> For the extremities of the earth, and all in every part of it who purely and rightly confess the Lord, look directly towards the most holy Roman Church and its confession and faith, as it were to a sun of unfailing light, awaiting from it the bright radiance of our fathers, according to what the six inspired and holy Councils have purely and piously decreed, declaring most expressly the symbol of faith. For from the coming down of the Incarnate Word among us, all the churches in every part of the world have possessed that greatest church alone as their base and foundation, seeing that, according to the promise of Christ our Savior, the gates of hell do never prevail against it, that it possesses the Keys of right confession and faith in Him, that it opens the true and only religion to such as approach with piety, and shuts up and locks every heretical mouth that speaks injustice against the Most High.[9]

The witness of the pre-Schism Popes, Fathers, and Councils (whatever the historical and theological difficulties encountered) was overwhelming in their cumulative impact as supporting the dogma of Papal Primacy as defined in the decrees of Vatican I.

The utterly supernatural nature of the Apostolic Primacy of the "first of Bishops," the Roman Pontiff, was profoundly grasped by the great 19th century German theologian Matthias Joseph Scheeben. His

---

9 P.G. 91, 137ff.

especially rich theological exposition was of particular value to me in dissipating the misconceptions of Orthodox polemicists. At a time when these same misconceptions concerning the nature and scope of Papal authority seem to have been revived among neo-Modernist theologians spreading dissent and disobedience in the Church in recent decades, Fr. Scheeben's remarkable exposition is worth repeating here:

> [T]he unity of the Church in its social life depends in a special way on the unity of the pastoral power. This unity of the pastoral power must be a clear sign that the Spirit operating in many organs is a single Spirit, who brings all these organs together in one whole, and causes them to exercise their activity in an orderly manner conformable with the unity of the whole. The members and organs of the Church form one body of Christ and assemble around the Eucharist as the source of their common life, and *they are called to image forth the highest unity of all, that of the Trinity.* In the unfolding of their life and activity, these members and organs constitute a closely knit whole, in which the unity and harmony of external social life is the faithful reflection of its true, internal, mysterious unity. *This fact must be manifested by the unity of the pastoral power.*
>
> This unity of pastoral power is guaranteed by the revealed doctrine that the plenitude of such power is in one supreme pontiff. . . .
>
> Owing to the fact that the plenitude of the pastoral power resides in him, and that no such power can be envisaged in the Church as independent of his, the Church is made truly and perfectly one, not only in its summit, but in its deepest base—and from the base up, not only in its topmost branch, but in its root—and from the root up. *Any other, lesser unity in the Church is unthinkable, unless the social structure of its social organization is to be at odds with its inner nature.* . . .

James Likoudis* (1928–)

The Church . . . is formed around an already existing supernatural center, namely Christ and His Holy Spirit, and this center must, by intrinsic necessity, manifest itself in the social organism in the person of a single representative, a single organ. The Church does not project this central point from itself, nor is the center set up by God merely for the purpose of completing the Church as an undivided whole. Rather, it is intended to be the foundation upon which the Church is constructed; by which the Church rests upon the God-man and the Holy Spirit, and by which the unity of the Church is not incidentally brought about or crowned, but is essentially procured. *The Church as a society is held together in this central point, as it is in Christ; through it the Church is in Christ, because it is only through it that Christ, as the supreme head of the Church, is in the Church with His pastoral power.* . . ..

[W]hy should we be reluctant to admit a mysterious foundation for the external organization of this structure [of the Church], whose entire being is a mystery? Why should not the Holy Spirit, who dwells in the priesthood with His marvelous fruitfulness in order to distribute His graces in the Church through its agency, be able so to dwell, and why should He not actually dwell, in the central point of the Church's social structure, in the bearer of His pastoral power? Why should He not bring the whole flock together in faith and love from that point, and through it impart unity and stability to the structure? Such union of the Holy Spirit with the [visible] head of the Church would be a tremendous wonder; but it ought to be precisely that. The Church is throughout an awe-inspiring, divine edifice. What wonder that its [Rock-]foundation should be so remarkable? The Church is the bride of the God-man. What wonder that it should be so closely united to Him through its [visible] head, and be so marvelously guided by Him through its [visible] head?

> *Only in terms of the mystery of the fullness of the pastoral office in the head of the Bishops, can we form an adequate notion of the sublime maternity of the Church.*[10]

I did not ignore examining the other Catholic doctrines (the Procession of the Holy Spirit from the Father and the Son, Purgatory, the Immaculate Conception, the Assumption, etc.) which had been attacked or denied by Orthodox theologians. Their objections were without merit and oftentimes Orthodox theologians disagreed with one another.

The basic self-contradiction and incoherence of the Byzantine Greco-Slav schism lay in its rejection of *a visible head for the visible Church Militant*. An acephalous hierarchy was a monstrous entity. The "undivided Church of the first seven Ecumenical Councils" was an historical fiction except on the Catholic premise of a hierarchical Episcopate having a visible head and center of unity with the supreme authority to call or confirm such Councils. The very *unity and infallibility of the visible Church* (professed by most Orthodox) could not logically be upheld without the admission of a visible head possessing infallible authority in faith and morals.

The great heretical and schismatic movements combatted by the first seven Ecumenical Councils had involved sometimes hundreds of Bishops engaged in rebellion against the See of Peter and the Bishops in communion with him. When Patriarchs and Bishops disagreed with one another over the most complex and intricate questions of dogma, how could a simple believer (much less scholars) possibly resolve the question of which group of Bishops had preserved the orthodox and apostolic faith? The "Eastern Orthodox" had no answer to that burning question. Catholics, however, had *a visible criterion* easily applied by any believer to determine where the true Church was—which group of Bishops had embraced schism and/or heresy, and which group was in continuity with Catholic Tradition. St. Ambrose had put it as succinctly as possible: *"Where Peter is, there is the Church."* The *visible criterion of Catholicity had always been visible communion with the*

---

10 Fr. Matthias J. Scheeben, *The Mysteries of Christianity* (St. Louis: B. Herder, 1946), 552–553, 555, emphasis added.

See of Peter. The true Church of Jesus Christ is always identifiable by its communion with the infallible Chair of Peter. Since the "cursed schism" with Rome, the autocephalous Eastern Orthodox Churches lacked that supreme authority with which Christ had endowed His Church to assure its remaining always One, Holy, Catholic, and Apostolic. In the 13th century, as Byzantine polemics against the Apostolic Primacy increased, the Angelic Doctor, St. Thomas Aquinas pointed out the disastrous consequences of negating the Petro-centric structure of the Hierarchical Church.

> And while they deny that there is one [visible] head of the Church, that is to say, the Holy Roman Church, they manifestly deny the unity of the Mystical Body, for there cannot be one body if there is not one head, nor one congregation of the faithful where there is not one rector. Hence, "there shall be one flock and one shepherd."[11]

The logical result of denials of the Catholic dogmas of Papal Primacy and Infallibility has been, sadly, the *abandonment of traditional ecclesiology stressing the visibility and infallibility of the hierarchical Church*. Thus, the Russian Orthodox Nicholas Zernov has written in Protestantizing fashion:

> There are not and there cannot be external organs or methods of testifying to the internal evidence of the Church; this must be admitted frankly and resolutely. Anyone who is troubled by this lack of external evidence for ecclesiastical truth does not believe in the Church and does not know it. . . . The ecclesiastical fetishism which seeks an oracle speaking in the name of the Holy Spirit and which finds it in the person of a supreme hierarch, *or in the episcopal order and its assemblies,*—this fetishism is a terrible symptom of half-faith.[12]

---

11 St. Thomas Aquinas, *Contra Errores Graecorum*, II.
12 Nicholas Zernov, *The Church of the Eastern Christians*, 1942, emphasis added.

Similarly, the Greek theologian P. Bratsiotis revealed the utter breakdown of the traditional principle of hierarchical authority once exercised in the "undivided Church of the first seven Ecumenical Councils" when he dared to write:

> [T]he supreme authority in the Orthodox Church lies in the ecumenical councils whose *ecumenicity must be recognized and witnessed by the conscience of the whole Church*. In other words, the decisive criterion of an ecumenical council is the recognition of its decrees *by the whole Church which is therefore, in fact, the sole authority in Orthodoxy*.[13]

By the above criterion none of the first seven Ecumenical Councils could be recognized as truly ecumenical since none received the adherence of the whole Church; each was rejected by large numbers of laity and hierarchy. Clearly, without a visible head of the Church able to confirm Councils as "ecumenical" in the name of "the whole Church," the very notion of an "Ecumenical Council" was rendered meaningless.

The above analysis was developed at far greater length as I sought to unravel certain difficulties encountered. Suffice it, however, to note that by my last year of university study I had become convinced that to be true to itself as well as to the simplest facts of Church history, Eastern Orthodox ecclesiology logically demanded belief in the Catholic dogmas of Papal Primacy and Infallibility. Belief in One Visible Church constituted by Christ as *"a people made one with the unity of the Father, the Son, and the Holy Spirit"* made historical and theological sense only in the context of a Primacy of supreme authority bonding in unity the entire collegial-episcopal structure of the Church. "Thou knowest that I love Thee," thrice repeated the Prince of the Apostles to the Risen Lord before receiving the chief authority in the Church (Jn. 21: 14–18). The Apostolic Primacy of Peter and his successors, the Roman Pontiffs, was also a Primacy of Love. This Primacy of fatherly love in the Church established by Jesus Christ, the "Lover of mankind," to endure perpetually in Peter and his successors had its

---

13 P. Bratsiotis, *The Ecumenical Review*, vol. 12, 161, emphasis added.

fitting exemplar in the effusion of love that characterized the Procession of the Holy Spirit from the Father and the Son.

Since I had reached the point by God's grace that I could no longer justify being separated from the *Catholica* (as St. Augustine described the true Church) built on the impregnable Rock of Peter, I took the opportunity to be formally reconciled. This occurred in 1952, shortly after I was inducted into the Army and before leaving for Korean service. Ruth had entered the Church even earlier, and we were married after my basic training ended. Needless to say, both our families were upset with our becoming Catholic, and with our marriage. We have always felt, however, that the Catholic Faith is "the pearl of great price" for which no sacrifice is too great. I have always looked upon my embracing catholicity and our marriage as among the greatest graces received in my life.

I pray daily for the reintegration of the Byzantine Greco-Slav peoples into Catholic Unity. Would that more Catholics did so, recalling that one of the major reasons for calling the 2nd Vatican Council was to achieve the end of that "lamentable schism"—a goal desired by so many Saints across the centuries (including the recently canonized (October 16, 1983) Croatian confessor St. Leopoldo of Castelnovo, OFM Cap). May God grant it soon through the intercession of the Immaculate Mother of God, Help of Christians.

Glory be to Thee, O Christ Our God, Glory be to Thee.

Part II—At the University
More on an Intellectual Journey
[Detailing results of the study of the history of the
Roman Primacy in the Church]

I recall with some humor that when I registered for my first Philosophy class at the University of Buffalo (when it was a private institution and before it became part of the larger State University of New York system), the instructor (a Unitarian-Universalist minister) informed the class that if anyone still believed in God, he should leave. I immediately took him up on his offer and walked out of the class, struck by the arrogance and smugness of a minister who had clearly apostatized from traditional Christian belief. I had never doubted the existence of God, nor that Christ was God. The all-powerful and majestic Pantocrator so vividly portrayed in the apse of Byzantine churches had always seized my imagination. Jesus Christ was indeed the all-powerful God, the Eternal Son of God begotten of the Father and of whom the historic Christian Creeds spoke and of whom the Scriptures witnessed with such forcefulness. While in High School I had been touched by the figure of Christ as recounted in the Gospels and such novels as "Quo Vadis" and "Ben Hur" had a particular attraction for me. Even a surface reading of the Gospels (whatever the exaggerations and artificial idealization of its main character hostile critics alleged to have occurred) revealed the existence of an extraordinary Man who claimed to be the Messiah and something much more, uttered prophecies, worked miracles, and engaged in establishing a Church which taught some mysterious doctrines.

Reading further in those Gospels (the latter appeared to me largely trustworthy as written by those who personally knew Him or His immediate Apostles), it was clear enough that the figure of Jesus depicted there was held to be the Son of God and that in a sense that no other human could make. The Gospels reported His claim to be equal to the Father, to be Himself divine, to be impeccable (indeed, "like us in all things but sin"), and to be mankind's Savior from sin. He would be condemned for blasphemy by His own people, would suffer the agonizing torment of Crucifixion only to be acclaimed by His followers as One Risen from the dead. Even as a young student I could not doubt that Jesus Christ manifested a human perfection, and a Wisdom and Holiness unsurpassed among all the leaders of religion. He was certainly believed to be God not only by the earliest Christians but by Christians in the Second Millennium throughout the Western world. He had spoken of His heavenly Father with an intimacy and certitude dared by no other Man in history. He was, moreover, to be loved and adored by His followers as no other in the history of the world. To His disciples, He had said, "Let not your heart be troubled. You believe in God, believe also in Me" (Jn. 14:1). I did so believe. I could not ignore His miracles or "signs" as recounted by

His disciples in the pages of those ancient writings known as the Gospels. They were astounding in what they related. Christ suspended the forces of nature, walked on water, healed the blind, the deaf and dumb, expelled demons from the possessed, and raised the dead from the grave. Even more astonishing was His forgiving sins by His own power and His claim to judge (as the searcher of hearts—Mk. 4:22) the world at the Last Day. Prophesying His own Passion and death, He calmly predicted His Resurrection from the dead. He had asserted power over His own life and death, declaring: "No one takes life from Me, but I lay it down of Myself. I have the power to lay it down, and I have the power to take it up again." He spoke of establishing a Kingdom not of this world but would be in this world as a visible Church against which the Gates of Hell would not prevail (Matt. 16: 18). One of His Apostles (St. Paul) wrote that this Church would be "the Pillar and Ground of the truth" (1 Tim. 3: 15) and He stated solemnly to His faithful band of Twelve Apostles that He would be with them even to the end of the world (Matt. 28: 20). In my reading about the greatest men in history, no man had ever spoken like that Man (Jn. 7: 46) and with such Divine Knowledge and Authority concerning the meaning of human life and the supernatural destiny of mankind. With the "crowds," I, too, was "astonished at His teaching for He was teaching them as One having authority, and not as their Scribes and Pharisees" (Matt. 7: 28–29).

Asserting without hesitation that He had "come down from heaven" (Jn. 6: 38), He claimed to be the long-awaited Messiah of the Jewish people and to "grant eternal life" to those who would eat His Flesh and drink His Blood (a reference to the awesome Mystery of the Eucharist which would soon be celebrated after His death, Resurrection and Ascension, on Christian altars throughout the Roman Empire). He declared Himself to possess "all power in heaven and on earth," thereby commissioning His Apostles to "make disciples of all nations" (Matt. 28: 19–20). He asserted without arrogance that He was "the Light of the world" (Jn. 8: 12), "the Way, the Truth, and the Life" (Jn. 14: 6), and "I am the Resurrection and the Life" (Jn. 11: 25). Regardless of the demythologizers of the rational Age of Enlightenment and into our own century using scissors and paste with a vengeance to discredit the historicity and credibility of New Testament writings and to create a Christ in their own unbelieving image, there was no convincing proof given to me to deny that the Christ presented in the New Testament conformed to the truth for which the early Christians were willing to die. The Christ of History and the Christ of Faith were the same. It was not without serious reasons that the Apostles and their followers had come to believe that their Master was perfect Man and perfect God. The dogma of Christ's divinity was to me eminently worthy of belief for, as that great genius Pascal is said to have observed concerning the martyrdom of the early Apostles and evangelists: "I believe those witnesses who get their throats cut." In his book *Mere Christianity*, C.S. Lewis had issued his challenge to modern skeptics faced with the witness of the Gospel writers,

> Either this man was, and is, the Son of God or else a madman or something worse. You can shut Him up for a fool, you can spit at Him and kill Him as a demon; or you can fall at His feet and call Him Lord and God. But let us not come with any patronizing nonsense about Him being a great human teacher. He has not left that open to us. He did not intend to.[14]

There was also wondrous continuity in the belief of the Church of the Apostles with that of the primitive Early Church and that of the Church of the later Ecumenical Councils. Whatever caviling the "historical-critical method" of German higher biblical criticism might make in questioning the factual credibility of the Gospels, it was historically indisputable that explicit belief in the divinity of Christ marked the preaching and teaching and liturgies of the Church called Catholic from its earliest days. Its rulers, Bishops occupying the Sees of the major cities in the Roman Empire, would by 325 A.D (the famous Council of Nicaea) hold fast to that primitive teaching and fix in clear terms the *homoousion* doctrine (Christ was of the same substance of the Father). This explicated the exact meaning of Christ's divinity

---

14 C.S. Lewis, *Mere Christianity* (San Francisco: Harper San Francisco, 2001).

as set forth in the Scriptures confided to the Church. The truth of the divinity of Christ who was "equal to the Father" but denied by the Arians was the fundamental truth of the Gospel, and Arius was considered a heretic from the very moment he began to spread his heresy, and this long before the Council of Nicaea. In the "Hymn of Orthodoxy" sung in the Byzantine Greek Liturgy of St. John Chrysostom, I would hear again and again the impressive summary of the Scriptures concerning "Christ the Lover of mankind"—the Christ who was the Incarnate Lord of Glory:

> Only begotten Son and Word of God, who art immortal, and didst deign for our salvation to be incarnate of the holy Theotokos and Ever-Virgin Mary, and without change didst become man. Thou wast crucified, O Christ our God, trampling down Death by death, being One of the Holy Trinity glorified together with the Father and the Holy Spirit, save us.

I have often felt that my Baptism into the life of the Trinity (as an infant in a Greek Orthodox church) had left in my soul an indelible belief in the Divinity of Christ, a belief that would serve to immunize me from the false philosophies of unbelief to which I would become exposed in my university courses. My own experience with "modern education" has shown that an indoctrination in Naturalism and Materialism and Skepticism only too often resulted from a purely historical treatment of philosophy. I saw students becoming confused by exposure to the contradictory systems of Spinoza, Descartes, Voltaire, the French Encyclopedists, Comte, Hegel, Hume, Kant, Schopenhauer, and Nietzsche, not to mention Dewey, Heidegger, and Sartre, as major philosophers who have helped shape the "Modern Mind" towards agnosticism and atheism. Then, too, there was the saturation in the anti-Christian views of such idols of the age as Darwin, Marx, Freud, Jung, or such popular writers as Bertrand Russell and H.G. Wells who were influential on campuses. In my own history and philosophy courses, I could already sense that a naturalistic and anti-supernatural Secular Humanism was in the process of dominating much of American intellectual life, and preparing the way for the rapid de-Christianization of American society and the collapse of moral norms we can now see affecting the lives of millions. In the late 1950's there were already intimations of the Sexual Revolution of the Sixties and the movement for a non-judgmental Sex Education in the schools of the nation which were to become a special challenge to historical Christianity's understanding of human nature and the meaning of human sexuality as given in Divine Revelation. It was the divinity of Christ that stood in the way of accepting any of the false philosophies of the day. Particularly helpful in assessing the growing unbelief of the 19th and 20th centuries was the book *The Divinity of Our Lord and Savior Jesus Christ* by the Anglican Canon H. P. Liddon who had observed in 1868:

> The vast majority of our countrymen still shrink with sincere dread from anything like an explicit rejection of Christianity. Yet no one who hears what goes on in daily conversation, and who is moderately conversant with the tone of some of the leading organs of public opinion, can doubt the existence of a widespread unsettlement of religious belief. . . . Their most definite impression is that the age is turning its back on dogmas and creeds, and is moving in a negative direction under the banner of freedom.

Despite Canon Liddon's inclusion of attacks on the Catholic Church and its alleged "corruptions in dogma" (a charge I was already well acquainted in reading Eastern Orthodox writers), his book was valuable for at least upholding the "dogmatic principle" in religion and refuting the attempts by Liberal Protestant theologians and humanist philosophers to "rob Christ of His aureole of Divinity." The writings of the early Christian Fathers of the Church he advanced further witnessed to the Divinity of Christ and, as I walked about the grounds of a beautiful campus, I found in St. Cyprian's words to his friend Donatus some words of consolation while reflecting on the growth of modern totalitarian and genocidal States which threatened the very existence of Christianity:

James Likoudis* (1928–)

> This is a cheerful world as I see it from my fair garden, under the shadow of my vines. But if I could ascend some high mountain, and look out over the wide lands, you know very well what I should see: brigands on the highways, pirates on the seas, armies fighting, cities burning, in the amphitheaters men murdered to please applauding crowds, selfishness and cruelty and misery and despair under all roofs. It is a bad world, Donatus, an incredibly bad world. But I have discovered in the midst of it a quiet and holy people who have learned a great secret. They have found a joy which is a thousand times better than any of the pleasures of our sinful life. They are despised and persecuted, but they care not. They are masters of their souls. They have overcome the world. These people, Donatus, are the Christians—and I am one of them.

But Christians were now sorely divided. How to account for that? How to account for the massive disregard of the Divine Teacher's prayer that all His followers,

> may be One even as Thou, Father, in Me and I in Thee; that they also may be One in Us, that the world may believe that Thou has sent Me. And the glory that Thou has given Me, I have given to them, that they may be One, even as We are One: I in them and Thou in Me; that they may be perfected in Unity, and that the world may know that Thou has sent Me, and that Thou has loved them even as Thou has loved Me. (Jn. 17: 21–23)

Did this not mean that the *oneness* of His Church referred not only to its invisible spiritual Unity but *also to its visible unity* which would be Christ's indelible sign to the world to believe in His Divine Mission? It was then that I began to attempt to resolve the question so disputed between Catholics and Eastern Orthodox concerning which was the "true Church" founded on the Apostles and which Christ had "perfected in Unity" so that unbelievers would believe in the salvific mission of Christ sent by His heavenly Father to redeem the world. I proceeded to read everything I could find in libraries that dealt with the Schism between the Roman Church and the Eastern Churches which had followed the lead of the patriarchate of Constantinople in breaking communion with the See of Peter. I also studied classical Greek for a year with University of Buffalo Professor of Latin and Greek, Fr. Michael G.H. Gelsinger, who was a convert to Eastern Orthodoxy from Lutheranism and for whom I had great respect. He had become a priest of the Syrian Antiochian Orthodox Archdiocese and engaged in translating liturgical texts. I still have the Prayer book that he composed for Eastern Orthodox service men. In the periodical he edited, "The Orthodox American," there was great insistence that,

> We believe in One Christ, and in One Church—the Church which Christ founded. That Church is the Orthodox Church. To accept the idea that two or more true Churches exist, is also to accept the idea that there are two or more Christs. The only escape from that conclusion is to deny that the True Church is a visible Body—a denial which in the end leaves neither a Church nor a Christ to believe in. If anybody says that it makes no difference what church one belongs to, he is really saying that it makes no difference what one believes. But if it makes no difference what one believes, then it also makes no difference if one has no belief at all in anything. If all beliefs are equally useful, they are also equally useless. . . . As far as Orthodoxy is concerned, only Orthodox priests are valid Priests. When Orthodox people receive Sacraments from non-Orthodox Clergy, they sell their souls as truly as Judas sold Christ.

In Lectures which he gave on the Creed, Fr. Gelsinger repeated at length that "the Orthodox Church . . . alone is the one true Church of the Creed" and "in so far as there can be only one visible Church, there are no sacraments outside of the one Church, nor any valid ministers." Of particular note was his commentary on the meaning of "Apostolic Succession":

James Likoudis* (1928–)

Apostolic Succession pertains to the transmission of the True Faith undiminished and unalloyed from the time of the Apostles to the end of the world. An unbroken line of succession for Bishops naturally accompanied the unbroken line of succession in the transmission of the True Faith unimpaired by novelties or losses across the centuries. Bishops are authenticated by the Faith, not the other way round. Where the True Faith is, there is the True Church. . . . . Of all necessities purity of doctrine is the very first one. . . . The unity of the Orthodox Church depends on three things: uniformity of doctrine, uniformity of canon law, and uniformity of ritual.

During his various pastorates, Fr. Gelsinger became deeply concerned with those he termed "Protestantizing Orthodox" who had fallen victim to the views on "reunion of the churches" emanating from the latitudinarian views of Protestant Episcopalians. He observed, "Indeed, so widely and so deeply has this propaganda taken hold among us that we behold the remarkable spectacle of Orthodoxy shattered into impotent disunity by unity propaganda." He worked diligently to unite the Syrian, Serbian, Russian, Greek, and Ukrainian Orthodox jurisdictions into one Federation. In his later years, Fr. Gelsinger would leave the Syrian Antiochian jurisdiction which he regarded as adhering to the "ecumenical heresy," and joined another ultra-Orthodox jurisdiction, becoming tonsured as the monk Theodore of the Great Schema in 1978 at Holy Transfiguration Monastery near Boston and dying in 1980.

As a Greek Orthodox I certainly agreed with Fr. Gelsinger and other Orthodox writers in repudiating the Protestant heresy that the Church was an essentially invisible body of true believers. Such a notion was practically unknown before the 16th century and absolutely contradicted by the traditional teaching concerning the visible nature of the Church held by both Orthodox and Catholics. To me, the over 30,000 Protestant denominations and sects only constituted a travesty of Christianity and the denial of any substantive Creed. They involved the denial of Christ's having established one visible

Church—the belief held in the first sixteen centuries by both Western and Eastern Churches. The great Dominican preacher Fr. Henri Lacordaire who helped revive Catholicism in France after its godless Revolution, had observed, *"The Protestant has not a single dogma to serve as a center of unity as a rallying point. He is his own unity."* After studying the writings of the Fathers of the Church, Cardinal Newman would write: *"To be deep in history is to cease to be a Protestant."* Where implemented, the basic (and untenable) principles of Protestantism (*sola Scriptura, sola fides, sola gratia*) had only led to the dismantling of Western Christendom and opened up the floodgates of the religious infidelity marking the emergence of 20th century totalitarianism. In contrast, both Catholics and Eastern Orthodox still believed—in Fr. Gelsinger's words—that the True Church constituted a *"visible Church which has had an uninterrupted continuation doctrinally and organizationally."*

However, I was quite aware that the notion there could not be valid sacraments outside Eastern Orthodoxy contradicted the teaching of St. Augustine (5th century) and that of the entire Western Church before the Schism as well as that of various modern Orthodox theologians who admitted Catholic sacraments to be valid and grace-bearing. I discovered that those Orthodox who held such a view (and still do) concerning the Sacraments were, in fact, sanctioning the mistaken and erroneous view of St. Cyprian that was adopted by the Donatist schismatics of North Africa whom St. Augustine refuted at great length. I wondered how the "Orthodox" Church could be said to have retained "purity of doctrine" in giving countenance to a doctrine that, in effect, declared the baptism and Holy Orders of the far larger Catholic Church invalid. Such an extreme view even unchurched the Pope (who would have to be rebaptized!). It was obvious that in this serious matter there was no "uniformity of doctrine" among the Orthodox. I would find this to be true in other matters of doctrine as well. As to the view that the True Church had to be characterized by "uniformity of canon law" and "uniformity of ritual," even my limited reading of Church history at the time quickly showed that long before the tragic Schism which solidified after 1054, there were distinct differences in canon law and liturgical ritual that did not affect the unity of faith between Rome and the various Eastern Churches. There was also the question of how the ordinary person could determine which is the True Church when scholars themselves disagreed on the content of the Faith taught by it.

Another very troubling matter began to give me pause. In reading the writings of the Fathers of the Church, both Latin and Greek, the Church was commonly referred to by them as the "Catholic Church." But I belonged to the Church known as the Greek Orthodox Church and could not help noticing the many Catholic parishes attended by Catholic people who belonged to the *Catholic Church*. St. Augustine who fought against so many heresies had stated in unequivocal terms that:

> We must hold fast to the Christian religion and to communion with that Church which is Catholic, and is called Catholic, not only by its own members but also by its enemies. For whether they will or not, even heretics and schismatics when talking, not among themselves, but with outsiders, call the Catholic Church nothing else but the Catholic Church. For otherwise they would not be understood unless they distinguish the Church by that name which she bears throughout the whole world.[15]

If St. Augustine spoke for the Western Church, St. Cyril of Jerusalem assuredly spoke for the Eastern when he taught his catechumens:

> When you go to any city, do not ask merely for the House of God or merely for the Church for all heretics pretend to have this: but ask which is the Catholic Church, for this title belongs to our Holy Mother alone which is the Spouse of Our Lord Jesus Christ, the only-begotten Son of God. . . . It is called Catholic because it is throughout the whole world, from one end of the world to the other, and because it teaches universally (catholically) and completely all the doctrines which ought to come to man's knowledge

---

15 St. Augustine, *Concerning the True Religion*, vii. 12.

concerning things both visible and invisible, heavenly and earthly; and because it subjugates unto godliness (or to the true religion) the whole race of men, both governors and governed, learned and unlearned, and because it universally treats and heals every sort of sins committed by soul and body, and possesses in itself every form of virtue which is named, both in deeds and words, and every kind of spiritual gifts. And it is rightly called Church because it calls forth and assembles together all men.[16]

I had collected enough Eastern Orthodox books and articles which frankly condemned the Catholic Church for its "heresies." (It became distressing to realize that the theologians writing them even disagreed on what those Catholic heresies were!) But people worldwide with no theological axe to grind (including some Eastern Orthodox) had no trouble identifying which Church was the Catholic Church. Efforts by some Eastern Orthodox writers like Fr. Gelsinger to establish the name of their communion as the "Orthodox Catholic Church" flew in the face of the historical fact that the venerable title "Catholic" was regarded by the Fathers and ecclesiastical writers as *exclusive* to the True Church and needed no qualifiers. Though the term "Roman Catholic" had an acceptable meaning (Catholics are those Christians in communion with the See of Rome), it was evident to me that Christ's "one and only Church" had been traditionally and properly known (and has continued to be known) simply as *the Catholic Church*. (In fact, so it would be later described and treated in the documents of the Second Vatican Council. The words of the Bishop of Barcelona, St. Pacian, were also crystal clear when he underscored for those seeking the true Church in the 4th century: "*Christian is my name, but Catholic is my surname. The former names me, the latter makes me known. Therefore by these names our people are distinguished from the heretics, we are called Catholic.*"[17]

Any further doubt as to which communion of Bishops was the "Catholic Church" of the ancient Fathers, Doctors, Confessors and

---

16 St. Cyril of Jerusalem, *Catechetical Discourses*, Chapter XVIII, 26.
17 St. Pacian, *Epistle* 1.4.

Saints was dissipated by reading again the Very Reverend Archpriest Michael G.H. Gelsinger, PhD's *Prayer Book for Eastern Orthodox Christians*.

In doing a research history paper on the early Papacy I recall the surprise I received in reading the volume *The See of Peter* by the non-Catholic historians, Shotwell and Loomis, which contained translations of the early Church writers and the Popes dealing with the prerogatives of their See.[18] I found I could not reconcile the claims of pre-1054 Popes regarding the supreme authority of their See over other churches with the endlessly repeated assertions by Greek and Russian Orthodox writers (such as the lapsed French Catholic priest, the Abbe Guettee with his book *The Papacy is Schismatic* translated by a Protestant Episcopal Bishop who similarly hated "Romanism"). The Abbe Guettee (whose volume continues to circulate and make dupes) strove mightily to show that all Bishops were equal in power and authority and that the Vatican I dogma of Papal supremacy was a perversion of a mere "Primacy of honor" the Bishop of Rome enjoyed in the pre-Schism Church. Among the many falsehoods and twisted history found in his book was the absurdity that "Hadrian I was in fact the first Pope." However, with the Shotwell-Loomis volume written by far more objective historians I was exposed to texts wherein the Popes long before the notorious 1054 quarrel explicitly stated their Primacy of authority over the churches of both East and West. In unambiguous language they affirmed that such authority was derived from the Primacy that Peter had among the Apostles. For these Popes (numbered among the greatest Saints of Christian antiquity), Peter had been established by Christ as the Chief and Head of the Apostolic Choir and made the Rock of the entire episcopate. These pre-Schism Popes[19] constantly invoked and alluded to the famous *Petrine texts* of Scripture[20] as the source for their unique authority in the Catholic Church.

---

18 James Shotwell and Louis Loomis, *The See of Peter* (NY: Columbia University Press, 1927).

19 Such as Innocent I, St. Leo the Great, St. Gelasius I, St. Gregory the Great, and those afterwards such as Hadrian I and Hadrian II.

20 Matt. 16: 18–19; Luke 22: 31–32; Jn. 21: 15–17.

I saw that Catholics and Eastern Orthodox were in general agreement concerning the role of the Episcopate in the Church. (This agreement, however, would suffer a serious blow among the latter with the growth of the Protestantizing Sobornost ecclesiology of the 19th century Russian lay theologian Alexei Khomiakov). Catholics and Eastern Orthodox traditionally held that Christ the Invisible Head of the Church had established Bishops in the place of the Apostles and made them collectively the teaching body which alone determined the dogmatic and doctrinal content of the Christian Faith. Those seeking the full message of Christ, the whole (Catholic) doctrine confided to the Apostles had simply to learn it from the visible Church built on the Apostles and which was indefectible in teaching and preserving the apostolic faith. The True Church was that which obviously possessed Bishops in an unbroken continuity from the Apostles and which taught the True Faith. The crucial question continually pressing upon me was:

Which group of Bishops (those in communion with the Pope or those in communion with the patriarchs of Constantinople and Moscow) was in historical and doctrinal continuity with the apostolic faith committed to that One Church? Both Catholics and Orthodox claimed to represent it. But as one examined the apostolic succession of the Eastern Orthodox hierarchy with its 15 and more jurisdictional divisions, one historical fact glaringly stood out: *Peter was missing among them.*

There was no answer to the question I would pose to those who maligned and calumniated the Papacy and regarded it as a deformation of the hierarchical organization in the early patristic Church. When patriarchs and Bishops divided on key (and difficult) questions of faith and morals, how does one know which group had remained orthodox? The history of the Church showed hundreds of Bishops deviating from orthodoxy and embracing heresy of one kind or another. Amidst the doctrinal confusion generated by the conflict among Bishops of famous Sees in the First Millennium, the Catholic answer was clear and unequivocal as expressed in the famous epigram of St. Ambrose (*Ubi Petrus, ibi Ecclesia*—Where Peter is, there is the

Church). The bishops who were with the Pope, the indefectible Rock of the Episcopate, constituted the teachers and rulers of the True Church, possessing the "Charism of Truth" from Christ to resolve dogmatic matters, such as, say, that other major dogmatic question of the Procession of the Holy Spirit which had exercised the minds of theologians (both Catholic and Orthodox) for centuries. True, the study of Scripture, the Fathers and the Councils would assuredly help in unravelling the difficulties encountered in the historic Filioque controversy which had seen oceans of ink spilt. But surely, I thought, there was no need to be an erudite scholar either to find the True Church or the true faith to resolve that doctrinal question. Moreover, falling back on one's own private judgment in interpreting the data of Scripture and Tradition smacked too much of the Protestant principle in religion and could not provide certitude. The question could be settled only by an appeal to an existing organ of doctrinal Authority in the visible Church which was both indefectible and infallible, but where was that Authority? Eastern Orthodox voices now specifically disclaimed the hierarchy's being the Church's infallible teaching organ. Anti-Catholic polemicists followed the Protestantizing Alexei Khomiakov in his outburst: "No! The Church is not authority, just as God is not authority, for authority is something external to us. Not authority, I say, but truth." But it was foolish to deny that God was authority. And had not the Risen Christ said, "All power (*exousia*) in heaven and on earth has been given to Me" and commanded the Twelve to "Go, make disciples of all nations, baptizing and teaching. . . ."? If Christ's words were to be taken seriously, they clearly manifested the transmission of His own authority as the Divine Teacher to the rulers of His Church, Peter and the Eleven. Not only did the Church's infallible authority guarantee the truth confided to it but it was from the infallible authority of that Teaching Church that the People of God were to learn the truths of Divine Revelation. The denial of the Church as an external visible authority amounted to a denial of the Church as a Divine Teacher by Protestants and rejection by the Eastern Orthodox of its infallibility.

Moreover, the very notion of Infallibility was historically linked only to the Catholic Church and its Chief Pastor. The 19th century had seen the explosion of rage of a rapidly deChristianized "modern world" at the dogmatic definitions of Vatican I. (1870) and against Blessed Pius IX who had earlier exercised that Infallibility in his defining the Immaculate Conception of the Mother of God in 1854. Infallibility (the supernatural gift of not being able to err in dogmatic teaching) had always been claimed as the peculiar prerogative of the Church's Chief Bishop who sat on the Chair of Peter as the heir of that Apostle whose faith the Lord guaranteed would never fail (Lk. 22: 31–32). Did not the ancient Byzantine Greek liturgy sing the praises of the Chief and Head of the Apostles?:

> *Of Rome made first Bishop*
> *Thou wert the praise and glory of the greatest of all cities,*
> *And of the Church, O Peter, the Foundation,*
> *And the Gates of Hell*
> *Shall never prevail against it,*
> *As Christ foretold.*

My examination of patristic testimonies had shown the special place of Peter among the Apostles and that of his successor, the Roman Pontiff, among his fellow Bishops. There was evidence aplenty in favor of the divine institution of the Primacy of Peter and his successor in the Church, and much from Eastern sources. Many of these have been collected and appear in the new edition of my book *The Divine Primacy and Modern Eastern Orthodoxy: Letters to a Greek Orthodox on the Unity of the Church*. Even a glance at the ancient Synaxarion of the Ethiopian Church testified to the headship of Peter in Christ's Church:

> And on this day is celebrated the festival of the honorable Peter, the head of the Apostles. . . .
> And because of this, Our Lord entreated him [Peter] kindly and gave him the Keys of the kingdom of heaven that he might loose and bind, and from that hour Peter became the head of all the Apostles. And he took the place of Our Lord in the city of Rome, and his position was above that of the chiefs of the world, and of Archbishops

and Bishops and Priests and Deacons and every other order of the Priesthood. Salutation to Peter, the Chief of all the Apostles, and of all the priesthood of the world.

Worthy, worthy, worthy is Peter, the Chief of the Apostles, to be the head and Archbishop of the world.

And having chosen St. Peter, He made him Chief of the Apostles. . . . And in him there was faith and zeal and love for God . . . and because of this Our Lord made him Chief of the Apostles. . . . Therefore, Our Lord [after his confession of faith] proclaimed him blessed and He made him the Rock of the Church, and gave him the Keys of the kingdom of heaven.

When all the evidence was sifted from the Fathers and other early ecclesiastical writers, from the liturgical books, and from the remaining Acts of the Ecumenical Councils as well as from the canonical literature, I could no longer doubt that if Christianity was divine, the Petrine office of the Pope was of divine institution (*traceable to the very words of Christ*) and of the essence of the Church's hierarchical organization. The Petrine Primacy of the Pope was the keystone of the hierarchical Church and essential for the preservation of its visible unity in this world. It was also necessary for preserving and expanding its geographic Catholicity as the Church commissioned to "teach all nations." It could not be ignored that since the Schism with Rome the autocephalous Byzantine Greco-Slav Churches had been rendered unable to spread the Gospel to the new peoples discovered in the Americas, Africa, and Asia. The Christianization of the vast spaces of Russia (Byzantine orthodoxy's greatest apostolic triumph) had actually begun and made progress before the Constantinopolitan Schism had solidified. There was no comparison between the feeble missionary efforts of Byzantine Greco-Slav Orthodoxy and the vigorous missionary activities of the Catholic Church that had expanded the apostolic faith into new continents.

I noted the more traditional Greek Orthodox writers who continued to speak much of Ecumenical Councils being the supreme authority and the infallible organ of the Church. But there were other

Orthodox theologians like Khomiakov who were to innovate by placing Infallibility in the whole membership of the Church, thereby rendering the very notion of Infallibility hopelessly unverifiable. The more traditional theologians, moreover, utterly failed to explain how one determines who even had the right to call such a Council. How does one determine which Bishops have the right to sit and vote in the Council when opposition may be registered by various Bishops to the Council being held or to its proceedings? How determine which Bishops have become schismatic and/or heretical when the consensus of Bishops is seen to have broken down and there results open rejection of its decrees (as with the great Reunion Council of Florence (1439))? Bishops are not individually infallible, and it is not clear how they can be collectively infallible without a head and center of unity whose supreme authority is acknowledged as preserving the collectivity of Bishops in the visible Church's organic and corporate Unity. As the Tradition of the Church discloses, Our Lord was known to have promised one Apostle that his faith would not fail, and the Church could not fail because it was built on him [Peter] as its Rock-foundation (*the visible image of Christ the Cornerstone*). Though some Greek theologians might still claim their assemblage of Churches to be infallible, in the last analysis they possessed no infallible organ that could voice a definitive consensus of all their patriarchs and Bishops on burning questions of faith and morals. In fact, the conclusion could not be escaped that the claim to infallibility by the Eastern Orthodox communion was bogus. No Eastern Orthodox I knew held that the Synod of Bishops of the Greek Church in Athens was infallible so that it could not err. Nor did I know of any Orthodox theologian who claimed that the Patriarch of Constantinople and his Synod or the Patriarch of Moscow and his Synod were infallible in the teaching of doctrine, or who held that any collective group of Patriarchs and Bishops could not err in the teaching of doctrine. The Catholic Church alone had a legitimate claim to be infallible because it actually possessed—in the words of Vatican II—an actually ruling Roman Pontiff as Successor of Peter and who was "*the supreme teacher of the Universal Church, in whom the Church's charism of infallibility is present in a singular way."*

In the writings of the great convert philosopher Orestes Brownson,[21] I had benefited from a powerful and detailed refutation of the afore-mentioned anti-Papal book by the Abbe Guettee which appeared at first so formidable. Brownson rightly declared "its spirit is ani-Roman, anti-Papal, full of venom against the Popes." Particularly noteworthy was Brownson's observation that there was no promise of the assistance of the Holy Spirit to any pentarchy of patriarchs in the Church or to a quaternity of patriarchs or to any Council save through Peter and his See. If the faith of the Roman See should fail, not only was there no reason to believe any Council infallible but every reason to believe that the Gates of Hell had indeed prevailed against the Church. A further study of the Seven Ecumenical Councils only confirmed for me Brownson's conclusion that "a Church really Catholic is inconceivable without the Papacy as the source and center of its authority and infallibility" and that "without the infallibility of the Pope, the successor of Peter in the See of Rome, the infallibility of Ecumenical Councils and the infallibility of the Church itself—could not be logically sustained."

The essence of what was to become Eastern Orthodox resistance to Papal authority in the Church may be said to have been plainly stated by the 14th century Byzantine Greek theologian and Archbishop of Thessalonica Nilus Cabasilas (†1363) who was the uncle of Nicholas Cabasilas, the famous writer of a classic work on spirituality *My Life in Christ*. In his work *Concerning the Authority of the Pope*, Nilus had written:

> As long as the Pope observes due order and remains in the truth, he preserves the first place which belongs to him by right; he is the head of the Church and supreme pontiff, the successor of Peter and of all the Apostles; all must obey him and treat him with complete respect. But if he departs

---

21 Orestes Brownson, *Collected Works: Vol. 5* (London: Forgotten Books, 2018).

from the truth and refuses to return to it, he deserves condemnation.[22]

Interestingly, English Protestants sought confirmation of their even more radical rejection of Papal authority. The difficultly posed Nilus Cabasilas' ecclesiology was that if Christ the Lord made Peter the Rock, Bearer of the Keys, Confirmer of the brethren, and Chief Pastor of the entire flock (and it was increasingly evident to me that He did!),—and that the same responsibilities were early understood to have been intended by the Lord to be passed on to his successors, the Bishops of Rome, *then how was it possible for his Rock-successors to depart from the truth in matters of dogma?* Writing earlier in the 12th century, the Catholic theologian Anselm of Havelburg seemed to me only to give voice to the Tradition of the Undivided Church regarding the prerogatives of the Roman Church. This he did in giving the details of his 1136 AD dispute with the Byzantine Greek theologian Nicetas of Nicomedia, one of the leading professors of the Patriarchal Academy. Whatever reservations Nicetas had towards the highly centralized Papacy emerging with Pope Gregory VII, he did not reject the appellate jurisdiction of the Papacy in the East nor did he deny the Roman Church's having some kind of appreciable Primacy in the Universal Church. Curiously, for Nicetas, the major problem harming communion between the Roman and Eastern Churches under Constantinople's sway was not the Primacy or Procession of the Holy Spirit. It was whether leavened or unleavened bread should be used for the Eucharist! This had also been the view of the early 12th century Patriarch of Antioch, John IV Oxita who had written: "The chief and primary between them [the Latins' and us is the matter of azymes. . . . The matter of azymes involves in summary form the whole question of true piety."[23] Only the most fanatical Eastern Orthodox would hold such a position today to justify a sinful Schism.

In Bishop Anselm of Havelburg's commentary on the Roman Primacy could be heard the echo of great Popes and Greek Doc-

---

22 "Peri tes tou Papa arches," P. G. clix. 728 D–29 A.
23 "De Azymis," 2.

tors (St. Maximos the Confessor, St. Theodore the Studite, and St. Nicephoros) of earlier centuries:

> The holy Roman Church, chosen before all others by the Lord, has been endowed and blessed by Him with a special privilege; and by a certain prerogative stands preeminent, and by a divine right has an excellence before all Church. For while other Churches at diverse times have been possessed by various heretics, and have wavered in the Catholic faith, that [Church], founded and consolidated upon the Rock, has always remained unshaken, and never, by any false and sophistical arguments of heretics, has been drawn away from the simplicity of the faith held by Simon Bar-Jonah; because it has always been defended by the shield of divine wisdom, through the grace of the Lord, against deceitful controversies. For it has never been shaken by any terror of emperors, or mighty ones of this world, because by the strength of the Lord, and the shield of a strong patience, it has always been secured against all assaults. Wherefore the Lord [knowing] that other Churches would be greatly harassed by the inroads of heresy, and that the Roman Church which He had founded upon the Rock would never be weakened in its faith, said to Peter, "I have prayed for thee, Peter, that thy faith fail not; and thou, when thou art converted, confirm thy brethren." As if He had openly said: "Thou who hast received this grace, that while those are shipwrecked in faith, thou abidest always in faith immoveable and constant, confirm and correct those that waver; and as the provider, and doctor, and father, and master, have care and solicitude for all." He rightly, therefore, received the privilege of being set over all, who received from God the privilege, before all, of preserving the integrity of faith. [Anselm proceeded to ask Nicetas of Nicomedia] "Why do you not rather receive the statutes of the holy Roman Church, which by God, and from God, and in the next place after God, hath obtained the Primacy of authority

in the Universal Church, which is spread throughout the whole world? For so we read that it was declared concerning it in the first Council of Nicaea by 318 Fathers. For it must be known, and no Catholic can be ignorant of it, that the holy Roman Church was preferred before all others by no decrees of Synods, but that it obtained the Primacy by the voice of Our Lord and Savior in the Gospel, where He said to Blessed Peter, 'Thou art Peter and upon this Rock, etc.'"[24]

If consistency in doctrine be the test of the True Church established by Christ, how could I deny the continuity of thought and practice concerning the Primacy of the Roman Church from the 3rd century on, when Pope Stephen was recorded as the first Pope to explicitly refer to Matthew 16: 18?

I could not ignore the remarkable continuity of thought and practice concerning the Primacy of the Roman Church extending throughout the First Millennium and afterwards (as with Anselm of Havelberg and later by the great Scholastic Doctors: St. Anselm of Canterbury, St. Albert the Great, St. Thomas Aquinas, and Blessed John Duns Scotus), I did not find the ecclesiastical history of the First Millennium supporting only a "Primacy of honor" that Orthodox polemicists condescendingly assigned to the Bishop of Rome in the obvious effort to evacuate a Primacy of supremacy that was of divine institution and one, moreover, supported by the Petrine texts of Holy Scripture. Then, there were the unforgettable words of the 3rd century martyr St. Cyprian of Carthage declaring in his Letters that the Church's unity was an *Undivided Unity* and such characterized the apostolic Episcopate ruling the visible Church:

> One episcopate, diffused throughout an harmonious multitude of many Bishops.[25]

---

[24] Quoted in Cardinal Henry Manning, *The Oecumenical Council and the Infallibility of the Roman Pontiff: A Pastoral Letter to the Clergy* (London: Longmans, Green and Co., 1869), 79–80.
[25] Epistle 55, ad Antonianus.

> Whereas the Church is Catholic and one and is not separated or divided, but is in truth connected and joined together by the consent of Bishops cleaving to one another.[26]
>
> For the Church is One, and this One . . . is not capable of being split up against itself, nor divided.[27]

To the mind of St. Cyprian, the role of Peter among the Apostles served as the type of the local Bishop being the head and center of unity in his local church. The schisms St. Cyprian deplored in his time resulted from disregard and defiance of the local Bishop. But there was more to his ecclesiology as he became aware that there were Bishops no longer in accord with each other. Though his tract on "The Unity of the Catholic Church" was directed at the evil of schism from the Undivided Church as represented by the local Bishop, he clearly acknowledged that the Roman See was the *"place of Peter,"* possessing *"the Chair of Peter,"* and served as *"the origin of the unity of the episcopate, to which heresy can have no access."* His concept of the Undivided Church was that of an undivided body whose Unity was prefigured by the Seamless Garment of Christ, and this made sense only if Peter were also the perpetual center of unity for the Universal Church. There were sufficient indications in the writings of St. Cyprian that the undivided unity of the visible Church and its Episcopate was intrinsically connected to the person of Peter made the Rock of the entire Church. *"There is one Baptism, and one Holy Spirit, and one Church founded by Christ upon Peter, as the source and principle of unity."*[28]

In commenting on St. Cyprian's words in his famous *De Catholicae Ecclesiae Unitate* that the origin of the Church's visible unity *"draws its origin from one only,"* Peter, Orestes Brownson once again showed the unreasonableness of Peter's successor being regarded as just the "first among equals" among his fellow Bishops and possessing a mere "Primacy of honor" in the Universal Church:

---

26 Epistle 66, ad Florentius.
27 Epistle 69, ad Magnus.
28 Epistle 60, ad Januarius.

> The Church is an organism with Jesus Christ Himself for its invisible and ultimate centre and source of life. But as the Church is to deal with the world and operate in time and space, it must be visible as well as invisible. Then the invisible must be visibly expressed or represented. But this cannot be done unless here is a visible expression or representation in the exterior organic body of this interior and invisible centre and source of unity, life, and authority, which is what Our Lord Himself is. To establish this exterior or visible representation, Our Lord institutes the apostolic college, and through that the episcopal body, through whom the whole flock becomes in union with their pastors, who are in union with the apostles, one organic body; but only on condition of the unity of the apostolic college, which unity must start from one, from a visible centre and source of unity. Hence Our Lord chose Peter as the central point of union for the apostolic college, and Peter's chair, the *cathedra una*, as the visible centre of union for the whole episcopal body, and through them of the whole Church, so that the whole Church in the apostolate, in the episcopate, and in the flock, is shown to be one, represented with the unity and authority it has in Jesus Christ.

Brownson further refuted both Protestant and Eastern Orthodox charges that the Pope was not the visible head of the Church and that he had no preeminence over other Bishops by divine right. With regard to their misconceptions of Papal supremacy, he noted that the Pope is not the "sovereign" of the Church (*Christ alone is Sovereign*). He is rather,

> the vicar or chief minister of the Sovereign. He governs the Church in apostolic unity, not as isolated from the episcopal body, but as its real head or supreme chief. . . . He is the chief or supreme pastor, not the only pastor, nor pastor at all regarded as separate from the Church. He

is the visible head of the Church united by a living union with the body as it is to the body to be in living union with the head. Neither can live and perform its functions without the other, but the directing, controlling, or governing power is in the head. St. Ambrose said, "Where Peter is, there is the Church;" but he does not state Peter is the Church, nor does the Pope say, "L'Eglise, c'est moi," "I am the Church." Succeeding to Peter as chief of the apostolic college, he is the chief or head of the Church. [Those who would deny his Primacy of supremacy] make the Church in the visible order as a whole, acephalous, headless, and therefore brainless.

The noted Italian theologian Aurelio Palmieri (1870–1926) who was remarkably conversant with Russian Orthodox theological literature also expressed with great vigor the convictions I had come to hold:

> It is a recognized fact that the Churches yearning from emancipation from the laity or the civil power cannot help instinctively feeling the necessity of a supreme head of the Universal Church. The moral necessity of the Papacy is a corollary of the composite nature of the Church, which diffuses the supernatural life of her Invisible Head, Jesus Christ, through the medium of a visible human society. Anti-Roman polemics will never be able to deny that a visible body needs a visible head. Protestants sincerely longing and working for unity admit the logical connection between a visible Church and its visible headship. . . . Russian Orthodoxy, which better than other Churches, preserves the true notion of the Church of Christ, can, only by fighting its own theological principles, reject the necessity of a visible head in the Mystical Body of Our Lord.[29]

Another writer who had a profound influence on me was the prophetic Russian philosopher Vladimir Soloviev who pleaded with his

---

29 Aurelio Palmieri, *The Catholic World*, vol. 104.

countrymen for an end to the "anti-Catholic Orthodoxy" which had led to the Byzantine Greco-Slav Churches becoming "paralyzed and dismembered." The only solution to the disorders which plagued the isolated national Churches of the Eastern Orthodox communion was reconciliation with the Successor of Peter. In his classic *Russia and the Universal Church* which was published in France because of czarist censorship, he published one of the most powerful works in defense of the Primacy of Peter and the universal authority of the Bishop of Rome in the Universal Church.[30] Soloviev noted how before the fatal Schism "the Greek Church was, and knew herself to be, a living part of the Universal Church closely bound to the whole by the common center of unity, the apostolic Chair of Peter." As the result of the negation of the Papacy by chauvinistic anti-Catholic controversialists, the Church had been sadly reduced to a "logical concept," an idealistic and "subjective abstraction" which gravely ignored the earthly Church's organic and corporate reality as established by Christ. In a stunning passage, he noted the necessity of a visible head of the Church to guarantee the freedom and independence of the Church from despotic temporal power:

> Throughout the Christian world only the Bishops of Rome have claimed their own see supremacy over the whole Church. The rivals of Rome, even when opposing the claims of the Papacy, dared not demand for themselves the same divine prerogatives. There is, then, in the Church of Christ, an historical centre which has never existed, either in Jerusalem, or Constantinople, or Moscow. He who disowns that centre of unity is logically forced to admit that either the Church is headless in her earthly life, or that her supreme government must rest in the civil power. In the first case, we would infer that Jesus Christ believed religious anarchy to be the best means of perpetuating His work amongst men; in the second, the Church would no longer be the universal society of the faithful, but a political

---

30 Fr. Ray Ryland, *Russia and the Universal Church* (San Diego: Catholic Answers, 2001).

tool, a department of a civil bureaucracy, suffering all the changes and vicissitudes of human policy and of human uncertainty. A single man, a man assisted and directed by God, is the granite foundation of the Church, and it is through that man that the Church states and formulates her authentic beliefs.[31]

Similarly striking was the view of no less a figure than the future heresiarch Martin Luther who, ironically, testified to the Undivided Unity of the Church grounded in the Petrine ministry of the Pope's visible headship, and this one year before his abandoning the Catholic Faith:

> If Christ had not entrusted all power to one man, the Church would not have been perfect, because there would have been no order and each one would have been able to say he was led by the Spirit. This is what the heretics did, each one setting up his own principle. In this way, as many churches arose as there were heads. Christ therefore wills, in order that all may be assembled in one unity, that His power be exercised by one man, to whom also He commits it. He has, however, made this power so strong that He looses all the powers of hell (without injury) against it. He says, 'The Gates of Hell shall not prevail against it,' as though He said, 'They will fight against it but never overcome it', so that in this way it is made manifest that this power is in reality from God and not from man. Wherefore whoever breaks off from this unity and order of this power, let him not boast of great enlightenment and wonderful works. . . . 'For much better is obedience than to be the victims of fools who know not what evil they do' (Eccl. 4:17).[32]

---

31 Vladimir Soloviev, *Russia and the Universal Church* (London: Geoffrey Bles, 1948 edition).
32 Sermo in Vincula Petri, , *Werke*, ed. i. 1883 (August 1, 1516), 69.

It was in reading Protestant authors after Luther (especially those who would be found fulminating against Vatican I and the *Syllabus of Errors* of Blessed Pius XI) that it became clearer than ever to me that their denial of the Infallibility of the Church and specifically the infallibility of the Pope as the Church's definitive doctrinal authority amounted to the nihilistic denial of Christ's founding a Teaching Church at all, thereby reducing Christianity to a jumble of conflicting opinions impossible to resolve with certitude. At the same time, I found the book *Doctrine and Doctrinal Disruption* by Protestant author W. H. Mallock of great value, for he confirmed with great power and logic the position of Catholic authors that a doctrinal Church necessitated belief in an Infallible Church. Without the Church being infallible and possessing divine authority to define its doctrines to meet future intellectual challenges, he concluded, "All doctrines are a fabric built in the air. . . . Without an authoritative living witness, the doctrinal fabric collapses"—as indeed could be seen in the history of all Protestant sects. Mallock insisted, moreover, that only the infallibility of the Church could guarantee an authentic development of doctrine. It was distressing to me to realize that the development of doctrine (which was an undeniable historical reality in the life of the Church) was something which all too many Greek and Russian Orthodox theologians denied as they did, increasingly, the Infallibility of the Teaching Church itself. In the following passage Mallock further observed that it was the Church's Infallibility grounded in the Petrine office that made possible the Catholic Church's singular doctrinal and structural continuity across the centuries:

> The fact that Rome is provided by the Roman theory [of Infallibility] with a teaching authority, which it never has lost or can lose, which is as living today as on the day of the first Council [of Jerusalem]; which is as ready to meet the scientific discoveries of the future as it ever was to meet the philosophic thought of the past, and which is destined, perhaps, to unfold to us a body of Christian doctrine wider and deeper even than that which it has already provided with an authority of this indestructible kind, is the feature

by which that Church is shown to be the one Christian body sill possessing the means of presenting Christian doctrine to the modern world as a body of truths supported by a system of definite proofs, and destined, like other truths, to develop as knowledge widens. This absolute continuity of authority only the Church of Rome claims in a logical and complete form. The net result of the Roman theory of the Church regarded as a witness and teacher of Christian doctrine, is to endow that vast body with a single undying personality—an unbroken personal consciousness.

It became crystal-clear that only the Catholic Church in communion with the See of Peter was historically credible as being the one permanent and infallible apostolic Church founded by the Savior, i.e., the one Church that was identical in faith, worship, and government with that of the Apostles.

By the time, therefore, I had graduated from the University, I was intellectually convinced that an indefectible and infallible Universal Church had indeed been established by Christ to bring all men to salvation. Moreover, Christ's own Headship of His Church-society demanded for the completion and perfection of its hierarchical structure the visible headship of the Pope if, indeed, His visible Church were to remain "undivided" when beset by schisms and heresies attempting to destroy the seamless garment of its Unity. In Colossians 1:18–19) St. Paul had written of Christ, the Invisible Head of the Church, that *"He is the head of his body the Church; He who is the beginning, the first-born of the dead, that in all things he may have the first place* [the preeminence—*protevon; primatum*]." If Christ is the head of the entire hierarchy of Bishops in the Apostolic College (as both Catholics and Orthodox asserted), the question was unavoidable. How is Christ's Headship and first place and preeminence represented in a hierarchy of multiple rulers and teachers of the Church? Where in the hierarchy is Christ's *supreme authority* signifying the oneness of the Church to be found? It could only be with one among the Bishops serving as visible head of the Church and thus "holding the first place" and being "preeminent" as the Primate of the Universal Church. To me,

Colossians 1:18–19 could not be enlisted in polemics denying a visible head to Christ's visible Church. The texts of Holy Scripture asserting the Christocentric nature of the Church rather demanded the truth of Peter's Primacy among and over the Apostles. It also demanded the continuance of that Petrine headship in an indefectible Roman Primacy as the center of the Church's visible unity if the orthodox Episcopate was to be preserved amidst schisms and heresies. Then, too, there was the overwhelming verdict of Church history which quickly revealed but one Bishop in all Christendom who explicitly claimed to be Peter's heir as the visible head of the Church and its Chief Pastor. Doubtless, the Primacy of the Pope as defined in Vatican I had undergone historical and theological development during the patristic and medieval periods and this in reaction to political and ecclesiastical vicissitudes besetting the Church, but this development was rooted in the supernatural Mystery of the Church with the Holy Spirit directing and guiding the Petrine office in its task of "confirming the brethren" (especially his fellow bishops) and safeguarding the "deposit of faith" from alien accretions.

The Greek Orthodox theologian Nikos A. Nissiotis had noted the grave defects of Eastern Orthodox ecclesiology:

> I do not know how far we can criticize Rome for its juridical Primacy and discipline, and yet at the same time remain passive in the face of our own failure to make our ecclesiology a daily reality of the life of the Eastern Church. Instead of one Pope we have silently accepted the many; instead of monarchy we enjoy polyarchy (and not the ancient oligarchy); instead of the Latin [sic] uniformity we have introduced national elements and ambitions. With no single governing head, each autocephalous Church being clothed with juridical authority, we tend to lose even the slightest, the most elementary kind of coordination and initiative. Our eucharistic ecclesiology centered on the local Church and her sacraments saves us from replacing the catholic [sic] by a universalistic conception of the Church, but at the same time we risk becoming the vic-

tims of our ambitions; these ambitions may spring from pride in the glorious past of our particular Church, or in the power of a Church seeking to impose its will on the others, or may use the Orthodox tradition to maintain the national inheritance in the countries of the diaspora.[33]

Other Orthodox theologians did not fail to note the consequence of the uncanonical fragmentation of the Church into phyletic national Churches resulting in the repudiation of the "universalistic conception of the Church." Jean Meyendorff lamented that "Our national, ethnic, or cultural commitments, while not evil in themselves, constitute real cover for 'de facto' separatism. They inhibit the missionary spirit, and hide the universal nature of the Church."[34]

Unlike the Eastern Orthodox dissidents' vision of the earthly Church as an autocephalous polyarchy (as many visible heads as there are Bishops with no supreme head or center of unity), it became clear to me that it was Catholic doctrine concerning the nature of the Universal Church which was a coherent organic whole in which Christ, the Holy Spirit, the Pope, and Bishops all fulfilled the roles which Holy Scripture and Apostolic Tradition ascribed to them. Christ was indeed the Invisible Head of the Church from which all supernatural life flowed into His baptized members, but the latter had been constituted as a visible body easily identified by its unity under a visible head who had succeeded to Peter's headship in the Church. The Holy Spirit as the Spirit of Christ indwelt the Church as its "soul" and was the giver of all graces and charismatic gifts making for holiness. It was the Spirit of the Father and the Son who kept the entire Church faithful to Christ's teaching via obedience to the rulers of the Church, the Successor of Peter and the Bishops in communion with him. The Holy Spirit held together in an indivisible visible unity the members of the Catholic Episcopate. True, the supernatural power of the Holy Spirit was the common possession of the entire episcopate but the head and members of this Apostolic College did not share it in the same degree. For the Successor of Peter possessed it in a way that

---

33 *Journal of Ecumenical Studies*, Vol. 2, no. 1, 60–61.
34 Jean Meyendorff, "Catholicity and the Church," [1983], 140.

made him the visible principle of unity for his fellow Bishops. The absolutely unique external visible unity of the Church reflected its internal spiritual and mystical unity resulting from the indwelling of the Holy Spirit and the abiding Eucharistic Presence of Christ. The pattern of hierarchical communion of Bishops with Peter's successor (*Primacy* and *Collegiality* in action) that distinguished the Catholic Church only mirrored that found in Scripture itself where one reads: *"And Simon and they who were with him"* (Mark 1: 36); *"Peter and they who were with him"* (Luke 8: 45); *"Peter standing up with the Eleven"* (Acts 2: 14); *"They said to Peter and the rest of the Apostles"* (Acts 5:37); *"Peter and the Apostles answering said"* (Acts 5: 29); *"Go tell His disciples and Peter"* (Mark 16:7).[35]

---

35 Emphasis mine.

POSTSCRIPT

On Church Unity and the Conversion of Russia Prophesied by Our Lady of Fatima[1*]

The writers contained in this volume bear witness with the Second Vatican Council that despite a profound and genuine communion existing between Catholics and Orthodox, such communion remains

---

1 * The following books on the Message of Fatima and Our Lady's apparitions in Portugal are recommended:
Fr. Andrew Apostoli, CFR, *Fatima for Today: The Urgent Marian Message of Hope* (San Francisco: Ignatius Press, 2010);
Francis Johnson, *Fatima, the Great Sign* (Washington, NJ: AMI Press, 1980);
Timothy Tindal-Robertston, *Fatima, Russia, and Pope John Paul II* (Still River, MA: The Ravengate Press, 1992);
Joaquin Maria Alonso, CMF, *The Secret of Fatima: Fact and Legend* (Cambridge: The Ravengate Press, 1970);
ed. Fr. Louis Kondor, SVD, *Fatima in Lucia's Own Words: Sister Lucia's Memoirs* (Fatima: Secretariado Dos Pastorinhos, 2002);
Cardinal Tarcisio Bertrone, with Foreword by Pope Benedict XVI, *The Last Secret of Fatima* (New York: Doubleday, 2008)

imperfect. For, as Vatican II reaffirmed, Catholic communion involves a visible unity of the Episcopate centered on the Rock of Peter perduring in his successors, the Bishops of Rome. That was the Unity which Christ established for his one, holy, Catholic, and apostolic Church. If Christ is in truth and not by a mere accommodation the Head of the Church, His headship in the visible society that was His Kingdom/Church on earth cannot be a purely spiritual and invisible reality. They became convinced that both Scripture and Apostolic Tradition provide ample evidence for the continuation of Christ's visible Headship over the Church through the appointment of St. Peter and his successors' exercising a Primacy of supreme authority among their fellows.

That Primacy was clearly promised to Peter by Christ's declaration, "Thou art Rock and upon this Rock I will build My Church." (Matt. 16:18); in conferring upon the chief and leader of the Apostles the Keys of the Kingdom (Matt. 16: 19); in giving him the singular mission to confirm his brethren (Luke 22:31–32); and to be the Chief Pastor of all His lambs and sheep (Jn. 21: 15–17). It was a Primacy designated to last as long as the Church itself.

It was impossible for them, then, to believe that the Body of Christ is still with us in a visible fashion, but that Christ, its Head, was not visibly present in the supreme head He appointed among the Apostles. Their separated Eastern brethren confessed there are many heads in the Church as there are bishops, but was there no supreme head who represents Christ in his teaching and ruling power? To them, the historical record was clear: The Fathers, Popes, and Councils of the Church held in the first thousand years attested to the unique and preeminent position of the Popes in the hierarchical structure of the Church. If the Church is the historical prolongation in time and space of the Body of Christ (as the Fathers of the Church taught in accordance with the doctrine of the Incarnation), then Peter and his successors in the Roman See were the prolongation in time and space of Christ as Head of His Body. It was true that the Church is a communion of particular Churches which are all apostolic in possessing the "deposit of faith" confided to the Apostles, but there is only one apostolic Church (*the Apostolic See* of Peter in Rome), that had received a divine promise from Christ Himself to never fail in confessing the Catholic and orthodox faith. No such promise was given to the Sees of Constantinople, Moscow, or other patriarchal and autocephalous churches, or to any combination of these.

Thus, to be incorporated in Christ means not only to be inserted into His Body by baptism but to adhere to the Church and its visible head, and it is in adhering to Peter's successor, that one is truly obedient to Christ. The solidarity, stability, and very identity of the Body of Christ under its Invisible Head, and therefore in its visible unity, holiness, Catholicity, and apostolicity, cannot be maintained across the heresies and schisms of history unless the visible presence of Christ in the visible head of the Church on earth is understood and acknowledged. The only solution to the problem of a divided Christendom for all who earnestly desire to be followers of Christ is to see Christ visibly present in the bishop who sits in the Chair of Peter and who serves as the Church's visible center of unity. This alone enables us to see how the Church on earth can in truth be His Body, since a visible body without a visible head and center of unity has no meaning. If Christ is still visibly present on earth, he is present in the supreme ecclesiastical organ He established for His earthly and mystical Body, and therefore there is never need to fear for the future of His Church. The voice of Christ is ever found in the voice of Peter whose faith cannot fail in his successors and who speaks for the entire Apostolic College of Bishops ruling the Church. It is the God-given charism of the Bishops of Rome to continue to unfailingly uphold the faith of Christ in all its purity and integrity; they will do so until Christ comes again to take back those Keys of supreme authority which have been their unique and heavy burden. It is also then that the Lord of History will come to judge the living and the dead and examine them for their fidelity to Him.[2]

All the Popes, from Blessed Pius IX (1846–1878) to the present successor of Peter, Francis, have prayed and labored earnestly for the restoration of Unity with the separated Eastern Orthodox Churches (not to mention the other Eastern Churches which are not

---

2 This summary of Catholic ecclesiology is based on a writing by Msgr. William R. O'Connor.

in communion with either Rome or Constantinople). The separated Byzantine Greco-Slav Churches have maintained a profound love of and devotion toward the Theotokos, the God-Bearer or Mother of God, Our Immaculate Lady. In the Byzantine Liturgy of St. John Chrysostom, the Blessed and Ever-Virgin Mary is acknowledged 16 times as the most holy of all God's creatures *"more honored than the Cherubim and incomparably more glorious than the Seraphim."* In Byzantine services she is profusely invoked as *"Our All-Holy, Immaculate, most blessed and glorified Lady, Mother of God and Ever-Virgin Mary."* In the liturgical calendar of the Byzantine rite there is a Marian feast for every day of the year and celebrating other events in her life on earth as well as the miracles attributed to her motherly intercession and help in all the needs of life in this "vale of tears." As Bishop Kallistos Ware, a well-known Eastern Orthodox scholar, has written: *"It is precisely on account of the Son that we venerate the Mother…When people refuse to honor Mary, only too often it is because they do not believe in the Incarnation."* Some years ago, Franciscan theologian Fr. Cuthbert Gumbinger, OFM, noted correctly: *"It is devotion to the Mother of God even among the dissidents that gives us hope for the reunion of the Churches. She, the Mother of the Good Shepherd, will lead back to the true flock those countless souls who, for so long, have been without a Chief Shepherd."* In his classic and still valuable work, *The Orthodox Eastern Church*, Catholic scholar Dr. Adrian Fortescue took occasion to observe:

> *The East has always exceeded the West in ardor of the reverence paid to the Blessed Virgin and the saints. . . . Most of all saints, of course, was the 'All-Holy Mother of God' the object of their devotion. Of all the generations that have called her blessed no one has done so with such eloquence as the Eastern Christians. And devotion to Our Lady is still a mark of all these Churches. It seems useless to bring quotations to prove what no one can deny.*[3]

As has been observed, for the Spiritual Pilgrims in this book, there was no question that their burning desire for the reunion of the Russian Orthodox Church with Rome would result from the intercession

---

3   Dr. Adrian Fortescue, *The Orthodox Eastern Church* (London: 1929), 102

of the Mother of God whose cultus was among the treasures of their Christian faith.

As previously noted, the Russian Orthodox patriarchate, the largest and most imposing of the Orthodox Churches, survived 70 years of savage and brutal persecution by the Communists, the *"enemies of God"* (as Pius XII termed them). Regardless of fanatical opponents of Unity with Rome in the various national Orthodox Churches, the ruthless persecution and martyrdom of both Catholics and Orthodox who gave their lives for Christ in all the Iron Curtain countries has resulted in an acute awareness of the sinfulness of their divisions and a longing for visible unity among those who honor the Mother of God as also the "Mother of the Church" and "Mother of Unity."

Our Lady of Fatima and Her Promise of the Conversion of Russia

It is astonishing as well as historically and theologically significant that the Mother of God so beloved of the Russian people should appear to three small children at Fatima in Portugal, in 1917 (even before the Bolshevik/Communist takeover) and promise the "conversion of Russia"—a Russia that would

> *spread her errors throughout the world, causing wars and persecutions of the Church. The good will be martyred, the Holy Father will have much to suffer, various nations will be annihilated. In the end my Immaculate Heart will triumph. The Holy Father will consecrate Russia to me, and she will be converted, and a period of peace will be granted to the world.*

Did Our Lady at Fatima prophesy a Catholic Russia? Such an eventuality would seem by human standards contrary to all human calculation given the centuries of division, continued theological and political quarrels, and remaining distrust and suspicion of the Papacy in Orthodox circles. But then it was contrary to all human calculation that the Iron Curtain would collapse dramatically in 1989 (*this was five years after the collegial consecration of Russia by Pope St. John Paul II on May 25, 1984!*). This was followed by the disintegration of the Soviet

Union, and the freeing of the Russian Church from seventy years of Communist oppression and centuries more of isolation from Catholic influence and direct contact with Peter's See. The chronological coincidence of the Fatima apparitions of Our Lady with the outbreak of the Russian Revolution in the days of October 1917 have often been commented on. The Fatima apparitions preceded by six months the explosion of the Bolshevik Revolution which would impose a horrific atheistic Communism on the Russian people. They occurred at a time witnessing divine intervention at the moment when the fate and salvation of many nations worldwide were placed at great risk. The Virgin appearing for the third time at the Cova da Iria to three little peasant children (Jacinta, seven; Francisco, eight; and Lucia, ten) on July 13. 1917, would mention the mysterious country *Russia* three times [four times altogether, including the last apparition to Sister Lucia]. The second part of the Fatima message spoken by Our Lady of Fatima and disclosed to the seer Lucia reads:

> The war [WWI] is going to end; but if people do not cease offending God, a worse one will break out during the Pontificate of Pius XI. When you see a night illumined by an unknown light, know that this is the great sign given you by God that he is about to punish the world for its crimes, by means of war, famine, and persecutions of the Church and of the Holy Father. I shall come to ask for the consecration of *Russia* to my Immaculate Heart and the Communion of Reparation on the First Saturdays. If my requests are heeded, *Russia* will be converted, and there will be peace; if not, she will spread her errors throughout the world, causing wars and persecutions of the Church. The good will be martyred, the Holy Father will have much to suffer, various nations will be annihilated. In the end, my Immaculate Heart will triumph. The Holy Father *will consecrate Russia* to me, and she will be converted, and a period of peace will be granted. In Portugal the dogma of the Faith will always be preserved.

It is worth noting that when the last living visionary Sr. Lucia (become a Carmelite nun) was once questioned regarding Our Lady's requests, she and the other little seers did not know what "Russia" was: "We thought she was a very wicked woman." Clearly, they were completely ignorant of the outside world.

What is absolutely remarkable is that during a war with devastating effects on all Europe, Our Lady is found confining her attention to Russia and calling upon the visible head of the Catholic Church to consecrate it to her Immaculate Heart. How extraordinary this was must be seen in view of the centuries of Russian Orthodox and other Orthodox Churches' polemics against the Catholic Church and the Papacy. The Roman Pontiff would be showered with such epithets as "the two-horned grotesque monster of Rome," "antichrist," "despotic tyrant," and "falsifier of the dogmas of the Church." The greatest of Russian novelists who was a friend of Vladimir Soloviev, Dostoyevsky, left an indelible mark on the Russian psyche with his novel *The Idiot* caricaturing the Roman Church. Moreover, in Chapter Seven of Part Four of the novel, it is the Christ-like figure of Prince Myshkin who denounces Catholicism:

> It is an unchristian religion . . . even worse than atheism. . . . Atheism only preaches nullity, but Catholicism goes further; it preaches a distorted Christ, a Christ it has calumnied and defamed, the opposite of Christ! It preaches the Antichrist. . . . The Pope usurped the earth, an earthly throne, and took up the sword, and since then everything has been going on that way, except that to the sword they have added craft, deceit, fanaticism, superstition, villainy. . . . Our Christ whom we have preserved and they have not even known, must shine forth in opposition to the West! Not by falling like slaves into Jesuit traps but by carrying our Russian civilization to them, we must now stand before them.[4]

---

4 Fyodor Dostoyevsky, *The Idiot*, pt. 4, ch. 7 (NY: Signet Classics, 2010), 567–569.

Yet, the beautiful Lady who appeared to the three peasant children at Fatima, informing them *"I am of heaven,"* brought a message of a supernatural nature that reaffirmed key doctrines of the Gospel revealed in and through the Divine Person of her Son. She confirmed revealed truths which were clearly of vital importance to the spiritual life and when the very thought of heaven and hell appeared to have disappeared from the consciousness of all too many people content to feed upon the husks of modern materialism and indifferent to the growing totalitarian menace of Marxist atheism. At Fatima the All-Holy Mother of God gave witness to the truths of Christian faith, one of them being the supernatural mystery of the Papacy, that is, Christ's establishing a visible head for His Church in the person of St. Peter and his successors, the Bishops of Rome. There is, therefore, nothing surprising that the Mother of God should appear at Fatima to manifest her love for the Russian people so dear to her and call upon the Roman Pontiff (who is, in fact, the Common Father of all the baptized) to consecrate Russia to the Immaculate Heart of Mary, promising to save it from Communist oppression by this means. *"In the end,"* Our Lady promised, *"my Immaculate Heart will triumph. The Holy Father will consecrate Russia to me, and she shall be converted."* The "conversion of Russia" clearly cannot be disassociated from the Roman Pontiffs' incessant pleas during the 19th and 20th centuries for the separated Eastern Churches to enter once again into Catholic Unity. They attempted to carry out Our Lady's request for the consecration of Russia to the Immaculate Heart of Mary. On October 31, 1942, Venerable Pope Pius XII consecrated the world to her, beseeching the Queen of Peace to,

> Give peace to the peoples separated from us by error or by schism, and especially to those who profess such singular devotion to thee and in whose homes an honored place was ever accorded thy venerable icon (today perhaps often kept hidden to await better days); bring them back to the one true fold of Christ under the one shepherd.

Later, on July 7, 1952, in an Apostolic Letter *Sacro Vergente Anno*, he explicitly consecrated the Russian people to the Immaculate Heart of Mary. Interestingly, Pius XII who died in 1958 was reported to have seen during the 1950 Holy Year "a miracle of the sun" similar to the one that occurred in Fatima on October 13, 1917.

His successors Popes St. John XXIII and St. Paul VI encouraged the faithful to consecrate themselves to the Immaculate Heart. So did Pope St. John Paul II who in 1981 and 1982 repeated the prayer of Pius XII in consecrating the world with solemn Acts of Entrustment. The 1982 Entrustment occurred when, filled with gratitude for Our Lady's intercession which diverted the bullets of an assassin thereby saving his life, the Polish Pope visited the great shrine in Fatima to thank her personally, and placed the near-fatal bullet in the crown adorning her statue. There he noted:

> In the light of the Mother's love, we understand the whole message of the Lady of Fatima. The greatest obstacle to man's journey towards God is sin, perseverance in sin, and finally, denial of God as manifested in the deliberate blotting out of God from the whole of human thought . . . the detachment from God of the whole of man's earthly activity . . . the rejection of God by man.

Nevertheless, none of the preceding consecrations by the Popes may be said to have fulfilled the wishes of Our Lady who had requested in an apparition to the visionary Lucia in 1929 a *collegial consecration* of Russia by the Pope with all the Bishops of the world. This was definitively accomplished by Pope St. John Paul II on March 25, 1984, in St. Peter's Basilica with many Cardinals and Bishops present. Making special mention of the Acts of Entrustment of Venerable Pius XII in 1942 and 1952, Pope St. John Paul II declared:

> We find ourselves united with all the pastors of the Church in a particular bond whereby we constitute a body and a college, just as by Christ's wish the Apostles constituted a body and college with Peter. In the bond of this union, we utter the words of the present Act, in which we wish to

include, once more, the Church's hopes and anxieties for the modern world.

With an obvious reference to Russia that had been made in the consecrations by Venerable Pius XII, Pope St. John Paul II declared: *"In a special way we entrust and consecrate to you those individuals and nations that particularly need to be thus entrusted and consecrated."* Did the Pope accomplish at that time the desire of Our Lady for the consecration of Russia in union with the bishops of the world? The Pope certainly thought so, the seer Lucia and the Bishops of Fatima thought so, as well as other Cardinals and Bishops and priest-specialists on Fatima. When on June 26, 2000, the Congregation for the Doctrine of the Faith (CDF) published the entire "Secret" of Fatima (with its First, Second and Third Parts), it left no doubt that the March 25, 1984, Entrustment by Pope St. John Paul II had fulfilled Our Lady's request for the collegial consecration of Russia. Unfortunately, this has not stopped the distressing polemics of those who deny it has been done or that all the Secret has been revealed. In his Foreword to Cardinal Tarcisio Bertone's *"The Last Secret of Fatima,"* Pope Benedict XVI may be said to have fittingly replied to such critics:

> John Paul II . . . was personally convinced that it was the 'motherly hand' of the Virgin who had diverted the bullet that might have killed him, realized that the time had come to dispel the air of mystery that shrouded the last part of the secret that the Virgin has entrusted to the three little shepherd children of Fatima. The Congregation for the Doctrine of the Faith, which preserved the precious doctrine written by Sr. Lucia, was made responsible for doing so. It was time for illumination, not only so that the message could be known by all, but also so that the truth could be revealed amid the confused apocalyptic interpretations and speculation that were circulating in the Church, disturbing the faithful rather than inviting them to prayer and penance.

If the faithful world-wide in greater numbers had heeded earlier in greater numbers the Holy Virgin's call to prayer and penance and acts of mortification for the conversion of sinners and especially the conversion of Russia practicing the First Five Saturdays, the conversion of Russia in the sense of the Russian Church restored to unity with the Church of Rome would surely have been hastened. Sr. Lucia herself acknowledged in a 1940 letter to Venerable Pius XII that with the collegial consecration of Russia "the days would be shortened by which God has decided to punish the nations for their crimes through war, famine and persecutions against the Church and Your Holiness."[5] What should be evident is that only the first phase of that conversion has occurred with the collapse of the Iron Curtain and Communist dictatorship in 1990. What has also occurred is the remarkable revival of faith in the former atheistic Soviet Union. In the words of the Metropolitan Hilarion (Alfeyev) of Vokolamamsk, chairman of the Department for External Church Relations of the Moscow patriarchate and who has often visited Rome to meet with the Popes:

> Over the course of seventy years, the Church was artificially separated from society; but after it left the catacombs in 1988, it became evident, despite seventy years of persecution, that it possesses enormous authority, that it is in demand, and that people await its return to public life. It is from this point that the Church's revival is taking place. It is taking place at a rate that is unprecedented in the history of Christianity. It might be compared with the period following the Edict of Milan, when churches began to be constructed everywhere within the Roman Empire, both in the East and in the West. We do not have statistics from that period. But we do have modern statistics. And they are very impressive. Twenty-five thousand churches have been built and renovated in twenty-five years. This means that one thousand churches were opened a year, three churches

---

5 See Fr. Rene Laurentin, *The Meaning of Consecration Today* (San Francisco: Ignatius Press, 1992).

a day. Eight hundred new monasteries. This phenomenon is unparalleled in church history, at least in recent history.

Many graces have been clearly granted the Russian people as a result of the collegial consecration of Russia made by Pope St. John Paul II. The greatest blessing is yet to come with a Catholic Russia rendered possible by freedom from the grip of Soviet Marxist atheism. One of the leading specialists on Fatima has written:

> Sr. Lucia has always thought that the conversion of Russia is not to be understood as being the return of the Russian people to the Orthodox Christian religion, rejecting the Marxist atheism of the Soviets, but rather as a total and perfect conversion to the one, true Roman Catholic Church.[6]

There is also the prophecy of the great wonderworker of Padua, the Capuchin St. Leopoldo of Castelnovo (1866–1942) who as an "Apostle of the Confessional" offered his 50 years of mortification and suffering reconciling sinners for the ecclesiastical reconciliation of the Eastern Orthodox. Aware of the appearance of Our Lady at Fatima and her message to pray for sinners, his confessional proved to be *"my East."* Croatian-born he dedicated his life and priestly labors for the return of the separated Slavs to Catholic Unity:

> I have the East always before my eyes and I feel that God wishes me to celebrate the Holy Mysteries, saving where justice and charity demand otherwise, so that the great promise of one fold and one Shepherd may in due course be fulfilled. And it certainly will be. This is what I think about it. God moves his ministers to apply his merits to the Eastern dissidents so that He is praying for them . . . and we know from His own words that God the Father always answers His prayers. The great event will therefore

---

6 Fr. Joaquin Maria Alonso, CMF, *La Verdad Sobre el Sacradoto de Fatima, Fatima sin mitos*, 2nd edition (Madrid: Ejercito Azul, 1988), 78.

infallibly happen. My task therefore is to work toward the realization of this great prophecy.[7]

The future is promising. It is assuredly the work of Divine Providence and prayers emanating from the maternal Heart of the Mother of God and all the Saints that there are now warmer relations between Catholics and Eastern Orthodox. This may be said to have begun with the meeting of Pope St. Paul VI and the Patriarch of Constantinople Athenagoras in Jerusalem in January 1964. Consequent visits of Orthodox patriarchs and Bishops to Rome and the visits of Catholic Bishops to Orthodox prelates have strengthened the bonds of friendship and represent the fruits of a genuine ecumenism. The travels of Pope St. John Paul II and Benedict XVI to such places as Constantinople, Cyprus and Greece have done much to lessen certain inveterate prejudices against the Papacy. The international theological dialogues participated in by Orthodox Bishops and theologians have also resulted in diminishing other doctrinal disputes (e.g., the Filioque) as obstacles to reunion.

It is well-known that Eastern ecclesiology traditionally favors an Ecumenical Council for the resolution of doctrinal issues. It is to be devoutly hoped and prayed that a future Ecumenical Council of Catholic and Orthodox Bishops (presided over by Pope Francis who is readily acknowledged by the Orthodox as *"the first of Bishops"* and who knows the Orthodox well) may be held and by the grace of God result in the Reunion of the Churches. Then *the concrete fulfilment of Our Lady of Fatima's prophecy concerning the conversion of Russia* will be realized. May every reader of this volume add their prayers for this holy intention.

Excursus:

Since the first publication of this book in 2016, a new conflict between Russia and Ukraine has broken out in February of 2022. Since then, Pope Francis has repeatedly called for peace and signaled his willingness to meet with Russian authorities to discuss what can be done

---

[7] Fr. Leopoldo of Castelnovo, letter to Fr. Odorico of Pordenone, his spiritual director.

to end the conflict including arranging to meet with Patriarch Kirill. Following the call of Ukrainian Bishops, the Vatican announced on March 15, 2022, that Pope Francis would make a solemn consecration of Russia to the Immaculate Heart of Mary, calling on bishops and priests around the world to make a similar consecration along with him in their own churches. Pope Francis made this consecration in the Vatican Basilica on the solemnity of the Annunciation of the Lord, Friday, March 25. While responses have varied, the Vatican has maintained their position that this act in no way repudiates the notion that Pope St. John Paul II's consecration was valid and fulfilled Our Lady's request. Rather, this new consecration was meant to call forth a greater abundance of grace and mercy from the Blessed Virgin Mary, who is a Mediatrix for mankind, and in order to bring grace and peace to a world torn by violence and strife. It is our hope that the republication of this book will help to bring Christ's light to a region of the world darkened by sin and death, that much good can be brought out of a situation otherwise filled with great suffering, and that those who read this book will be converted to help bring about a long-awaited Catholic Russia!

Index

A.
Alonso, Fr. Joaquin Maria, 12, 191, 202
Alivisatos, Hamilcar, 150
Anthimus, Patriarch of Constantinople, 148
Anselm of Havelburg, 178-180
Aquinas, St. Thomas, 147-148, 157, 180
Athenagoras, Patriarch of Constantinople, 203
Augustine, St., 21, 49, 53, 61, 159, 168-169

B.
Balthasar, Hans Urs von, 57, 61
Basil, St., 25
Bennigsen, Count George, 77, 127-143
Berdaiev, Nicholas, 66, 103, 118
Beshoner, Jeffrey Bruce, 33, 45-46, 49-50
Bessarion of Nicaea, Cardinal, 7
Billington, James H., 30, 57, 60
Boniface I, Pope, 151
Bratsiotis, P., 158
Brownson, Orestes, 177, 181-182
Bulgakov, Sergius, Fr., 66, 132, 134, 137, 140

C.
Cabasilas, Nilus, 129, 177-178
Calavassy, Bishop Georges, 114-115
Cerularius, Patriarch Michael of Constantinople, 90-91
Chaadayev, Peter, 46-47
Chrysostom, St. John, 53, 65, 78, 108
Collegial consecration of Russia, 15, 195, 199, 202
Constantine XI, Emperor, 17
Cyprian, Bishop of Carthage, St., 89, 164, 168, 180-181
Cyril of Jerusalem, St., 169-170
Custine, Marquis de, 28, 47, 49

D.
Daujat, Jean, 99, 103
De Maistre, Count Joseph, 31-33, 49-50
Dostoyevsky, Fyodor, 55, 59, 66, 119, 122, 197
Dudley, Fr. Owen, 147
Dvornik, Fr. Francis, 150

E.
Ethiopian Synaxarion, 174

F.
Feodorov, Blessed Leonid, 68-69, 71, 77-86, 119, 124
Filioque, 50-51, 55, 64, 71, 90, 113, 121, 150, 173, 203
Florence, Council of (1439), 7, 18, 55, 63, 114, 129, 150, 176
Fortescue, Adrian, 194
Foyer Oriental Chretien, 87, 93

G.

Gagarin, Ivan Sergievich, SJ, 28, 31, 39, 45-56
Gelasius I, Pope, 152, 171
Gelsinger, Fr. Michael G.H., 166-168, 170-171
Gennadius, Patriarch of Constantinople, 63
Georgiadis, Helle Elpiniki, 107-115
Ghika, Prince Vladimir, 99-106
Golitsyn, Prince Theodore, 37
Golitsyn, Princess Alexis, 31
Guettee, Abbe Rene, 53, 171, 177
Gumbinger, Fr. Cuthbert, OFM, 194

H.

Hilarion, Metropolitan of Vokolamamsk, 201

I.

Irenaeus of Lyons, St., 61, 65, 89
Isvolsky, Fr., 134, 143
Iswolsky, Helene, 45, 57, 68, 117-126

J.

John Paul II, Pope, St., 58, 85, 94, 191, 195, 199-204
Justinian I, Emperor, 17-18, 91

K.

Kent, W.J., O.S.C., 74-75
Khomiakov, Alexei, 23, 53, 137, 172-173, 176
Krylenko, N.V., 82-84

L.

Laurentin, Rene, 201
Leo the Great, Pope, 151, 171
Leopoldo of Castelnovo, "Apostle of the Confessional", St., 2, 159, 202-203
Lewis, C.S., 162
Liddon, Canon H.P., 164
Likoudis, James, 11-12, 15, 17-25, 87, 145-190, 208
Luther, Martin, 185-186
Lyons, Council of (1274), 18

M.

McCullagh, Captain Francis, 82
Macarius, Archbishop of Kharkov, 136
Mailleux, Paul, SJ, 69, 71, 77-80, 83, 85
Mallock, W.H, 186
Maritain, Jacques, 103, 118, 123-125
Mark of Ephesus, 63
Matual, David, 45, 53, 72-73
Meletios, Patriarch of Alexandria, 139

N.

Newman, John Henry Cardinal, 60, 63, 74, 147, 149, 168
Nicholas I, Czar, 37, 47, 50
Nicholas II, Czar, 80, 117
Nissiotis, Nikos A., 188

P.

Palmer, William of Magdalen College, 136
Palmieri, Aurelio, 12, 19, 64, 183
Photius, Patriarch of Constantinople, 89, 91, 150
Pius XI, Pope, 186, 196
Pius XII, Venerable, Pope, 7, 93, 108, 148, 195, 198-201
Posnov, Dr. Irene, 87-97
Posnov, Mikhail E., 88

R.

Ravignon, Fr. Francis Xavier de, SJ, 36, 49
Roncalli, Angelo Giuseppe, Apostolic Nuncio, 92
Rosanov, Vassilij V., 122
Rupp, Jean, Bishop of Monaco, 87-88
Rutt, Joan, 107

S.

Saint-Beuve, Charles, 49
Samarine, George, 45, 50-52
Scheeben, Matthias J., Fr., 153-154, 156
Schouvalov, Count Gregory, 35-43, 49-50, 80
Scott, S.H., 149
Sheptytsky, Metropolitan Andrew, 77, 79, 81
Shotwell and Loomis, *The See of Peter*, 171
Soloviev, Vladimir, 11, 15, 55, 57-68, 71, 78-79, 82, 119-122, 124-126, 136, 144, 151, 183-185, 197

Sr. Lucia, 12, 94, 197, 200-202
Swetchine, Madame Sophie, 27-34, 36-37, 49, 70, 80

T.

The Third Hour, 120, 124-125
Tjaer, Marguerite, 119
Tolstoy, Alexandra, 123
Tolstoy, Fr. Nicholas, 63, 119
Tondini, Fr. Caesar de Quarenghi, 40-41, 43
Transubstantiation, doctrine of, 139
Tsankov, Stepan, 134-135, 138-139

V.

Volkonskaia, Princess Elizabeth, 24, 69-75
Volkonskaia, Prince Alexander, 70

W.

Ware, Bishop Kallistos, 194
Walton, Leonard, 58

Z.

Zernov, Nicholas, 157

About the Author

A convert from Greek Orthodoxy, James Likoudis is an internationally known theologian and apologist who has dedicated his life to reconciling his Eastern Orthodox brethren with the Catholic Church Jesus Christ founded. He excels in analyzing the key issues that separate Catholics and Orthodox, including regarding Papal and conciliar history, and he cherishes all we hold in common in Christ. His passion and acumen are on full display in this newly revised edition of his most recent work: *Heralds of a Catholic Russia*.

Likoudis served for more than twenty-five years at the lay apostolate Catholics United for the Faith (CUF), including as president. His other books include *The Pope, The Council, and The Mass*; *The Divine Primacy of the Bishop of Rome and Modern Eastern Orthodoxy*; *Eastern Orthodoxy and the See of Peter*; *Ending the Byzantine Greek Schism*; and *The Divine Mosaic*.

He has written and lectured widely on ecumenism, religious education, the liturgy, sex education, family life, and the role of the laity in the Church. He is also a former college instructor in history and government, with more than twenty years of teaching experience. Likoudis received an honorary Doctorate of Divinity from Sacred Heart Major Seminary in Detroit (2020). He and his wife Ruth have six children, thirty-five grandchildren, and forty-four great-grandchildren. More from the author can be found at www.jameslikoudispage.com.

About the Editor

Andrew Likoudis, the grandson of James Likoudis, is a Catholic, entrepreneur, and studies business administration. He has held economics and marketing fellowships with Johns Hopkins University and Goldman Sachs *10,000 Small Businesses*, and is the Young Adult Representative for the Archdiocese of Baltimore. He is also a member of the International Marian Association, and the Fellowship of Catholic Scholars, and an associate member of the Society for Catholic Liturgy. He enjoys study of the intersection of faith and culture, and has edited five works on Catholic ecclesiology and the Papacy.